Ne

Muriel Dreifuss
and
Max Block

Contents

This Way New York 3

Flashback 6

Sightseeing 13

Downtown 14

Ethnic New York 20

Midtown 27

Uptown 35

Other Boroughs 46

Dining Out 50

Entertainment 61

The Hard Facts 66

Index 79

Maps

Midtown Manhattan	74–75
New York City	76–77
Greenwich Village	78
Manhattan	*fold-out*
Central Park	*fold-out*
Subway	*fold-out*

▌*Page 1: Reaching for the sky.*

The World's City

Whether you approach it by sea or by air, New York is one of those rare cities that can inspire love at first sight. There comes a particular moment when that stunning Manhattan skyline suddenly comes into view, when its familiar image converges abruptly with the stark reality of its glittering buildings. Pause on the threshold of one of the greatest cities on earth, a city that is at once exhilarating, overwhelming, bewildering and mysterious. Within minutes, you find yourself hurtling through a tunnel or over a bridge—any of the many concrete and steel arteries that pump its lifeblood into the island-city—until you stand, awestruck, in the midst of this amazing creation.

All its museums, restaurants, cafés and monuments notwithstanding, Manhattan is, first and foremost, testament to mankind's curious habit of living in close proximity to… other humans. You are surrounded by the mad procession of cars, the cacophony of horns, the blur of city lights and hectic throngs of people. It won't take long to realise that, while you've come to see a thriving American city, what

will greet you is the world. Welcome to the Big Apple!

The constant influx of energy, creativity and ingenuity from other shores has set this city apart. New York is home to some 2 million foreigners. In other words, one in every four persons living in Manhattan, the Bronx, Queens, Staten Island or Brooklyn was born in another country. More than 120 languages are spoken here, including Hindi, Arabic, Hebrew, Punjabi and Thai, and some 50 major religions are practised in 3,500 churches, temples, synagogues, mosques and cathedrals. Every year, dozens of parades celebrate the different cultural heritages of various immigrant communities.

The physical New York, as well, is a blend of immigrant flavours: a Swiss businessman bankrolled the Guggenheim Museum, a German immigrant engineered the Brooklyn Bridge, three Englishmen devised the grid system for the streets in Manhattan, a Chinese designed the Jacob Javits Convention Center and a Scot provided the funds for Carnegie Hall. The political landscape has also been influenced by the city's ethnic diversity: since the 1970s, a Jew, an Italian-American, an African-American and an Irish-American have been mayor of New York. In the last mayoral election of the 20th century, a black, a Jewish woman, a Puerto-Rican and an Italian-American—Rudolph Giuliani—competed for the city's highest office.

There is no question that the constant inflow of immigrants is what allows New York its penchant for reinvention, its uncanny ability to transform itself overnight, to maintain its energy, its vitality, its colour and its warmth.

What First?

New York City is home to dozens of magnificent museums, more skyscrapers than any other city in the world, thousands of restaurants, hundreds of theatres, the busiest harbour in the US. There is so much to see and do, that the most difficult problem you will have to face is deciding where to go first.

It's a good idea to get right down to business and take in the stunning panoramic view from the observation deck of the Empire State Building. Alternatively, you can catch the ferry out to the Statue of Liberty and imprint the Manhattan skyline on your memory. Perhaps you prefer a Broadway show? Be sure to look for the discount tickets on sale in Times Square. And if you're feeling adventurous, you can try some experimental theatre in the West Village. Music? For starters, listen to some great jazz at the Village Vanguard on Seventh Avenue, or fantastic blues at The Blue Note on West 3rd Street.

Of course, you might want to go shopping first. If it's clothes you're interested in, stroll over to Saks on Lexington Avenue and have a look at the latest designs in big-name fashion. Want to bring some discs back home? Hop over to Times Square where you'll find one of the largest selections of recorded music on the planet. And don't leave without visiting a museum. There's a bounty of them on Fifth Avenue; indeed, the stretch between 70th and 103rd streets is called "Museum Mile". The Metropolitan Museum of Art, the Guggenheim, the Whitney and the Museum of Modern Art are all within walking distance of one another.

Maybe you would like to do something out of the ordinary, like playing chess in one of the oldest parks in the city. Jump into the next cab and head over to Washington Square. There, in the southwest corner of the park, you can match wits with a Ukrainian pillow-maker, a Haitian trumpeter or a Japanese stockbroker. West of the park, on the corner of Sixth Avenue and 4th St, you can watch some of the best street basketball in the city.

By now you're probably thinking it's time to eat. The food! Afghan, African, Argentinian, Belgian, Brazilian, Burmese, Cambodian, Chilean, Chinese, Cuban, French, Ethiopian, Greek, Indian, Jamaican, Lebanese, Malaysian, Mexican, Moroccan, Peruvian, Polish, Russian, Sri Lankan… it's a culinary bonanza! You'll have your pick of everything from tasty French cuisine or Tuscan specialities to deli sandwiches bursting at the seams and juicy barbecued ribs. Don't want meat? There are places where the selection of salads is almost as long as the list of main courses.

Rubbing Shoulders with the World

Regardless of what you do in New York, you're bound to have a good time. And wherever you go, you'll be rubbing shoulders with people from all over the world, hearing their languages, tasting their foods, looking at their beautiful faces. New York will leave you with the unmistakable impression that you've witnessed a bit of every country on earth. And, in more senses than one, you have.

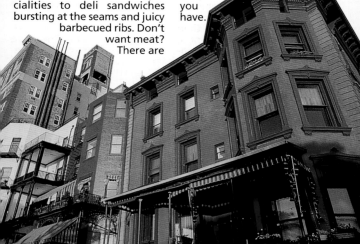

Flashback

As you make your way past the shops on Fifth Avenue and the outdoor cafés in Greenwich Village, consider this: the ground you are walking on was once dense forest. Thick shrubs and berry plants, creeks and ponds dotted the island. Deer, raccoons, wolves and foxes foraged inland, while turtles, salamanders, toads and frogs thrived near the marshes and swamps. Oysters were abundant in the shallows surrounding the island; dozens of species of birds lived in the overhead canopy of trees. And throughout, in small communities of grass long-houses surrounded by farmland, Indian tribes traded, cultivated crops, celebrated religious festivals, raised families and fashioned intricate tools. It was, indeed, a natural paradise.

Discovery

The Manates, a small tribe of Algonquian Indians, greeted the Italian explorer Giovanni da Verrazano when he landed in 1524 at what is now Staten Island. Verrazano stirred up appreciable interest upon his return to France, but colonization of the New World would have to wait. The treacherous voyage across the Atlantic, the danger of battles with the natives and diplomatic tangles between the European powers prevented any serious conquest of North America for the next century.

In 1609, the Englishman Henry Hudson sailed into what is now New York Harbor. He had been sent by the Dutch, in hopes of discovering a westerly route to India. Impressed with the furs, fruit and tobacco that Hudson brought back, the Dutch West India Company secured a charter to set up a colony on Manhattan Island and, in 1624, thirty Protestant families arrived in the newly bequeathed New Amsterdam at the southern tip of the island. Three years later, the Manates sold the island to Peter Minuit, the first governor of the colony, for the now famously insignificant sum of $24 worth of beads and clothing.

Setting Down Roots

Constant battles with the natives, and a young government that couldn't decide if it was running a business or a colony, were obstacles that the Dutch settlers struggled to overcome. In 1664, the British elbowed their way into New

Amsterdam—with little resistance on the part of the Dutch —and New York was born. And the Manates? By the time the British arrived, the 2,000-year-old native society had been virtually obliterated by smallpox, malaria, alcohol and the unsettling habit of the Dutch to periodically slaughter their new neighbours.

The British had a much better time of it than the Dutch. Under their supervision, New York became a powerful centre of trade, supplying Europe with furs, tobacco, sugar and tea. The foundations of a proper city were established during the hundred-year period of British control: libraries and theatres were opened, King's College—the precursor to Columbia University—was founded, a municipal government with a mayor was installed, the first daily newspaper was published, and streets, houses, businesses and public buildings stretched further north. By 1770, the population had grown to 20,000, consisting primarily of the English, the remnants of the Dutch community and roughly 1,500 African slaves. Treatment of the slaves, particularly under British rule, was harsh. Usually forced to work as domestic servants, they were barred from owning property, prevented from socializing in groups of more than three and forced to obey a curfew. If even a rumour of rebellion reached British ears, the slaves were often brutally punished or even executed.

Unrest

In an effort to subsidize their vast empire, the British parliament levied heavy taxes on the colonies in the New World. By 1775, the colonists had grown tired of sending their hard-earned money back to England. The struggle for independence began. There was a considerable effort on the part of the colonial Patriots to expel the English from New York throughout the war, but the Royal Navy had surrounded Manhattan Island. During the American Revolution, New York remained under British control.

His Majesty's troops surrendered in 1781, and the English began to leave New York two years later. But the colonists found their home in complete disarray at the close of the war. Much of the city had been destroyed during the fighting, there was little revenue as most trade had been suspended, and the sudden return to New York of thousands of Patriot soldiers presented serious problems. A housing shortage, poverty, disease and general discontent seized the city as it entered the 19th century.

Rebuilding

James Duane, the first mayor after the war, helped lift New York out of this dire situation. Docks and wharves were built along the East River to provide better anchorage for ships and encourage trading along the Atlantic coast. Streets were improved and sewers installed. A banking centre in the Wall Street area was constructed, together with a new City Hall. By 1800 New York had re-established itself as a strong hub of trade and commerce.

The completion in 1825 of the Erie Canal—a waterway connecting the Hudson River and the Great Lakes—affirmed New York's status as a major seaport and manufacturing centre. Goods were now more easily sold and transported to the west, and whatever New York City could not produce itself (coal, for instance) was shipped in via the canal. Sugar, flour, liquor and clothing were major exports during this period, spurring manufacturing and creating jobs. Expansion took hold of the city like a hurricane. Many of the original Dutch houses

WATCHTOWER

were torn down to make room for shops and banks, streets were widened and began stretching ever further north, and opulent private residences sprang up. Central Park was built, St Patrick's Cathedral completed and wealthy families like the Rockefellers, the Vanderbilts, the Fricks and the Carnegies assured themselves a place in New York's aristocracy by amassing huge fortunes, building palatial mansions along Fifth Avenue and throwing lavish parties.

A Working Community

The commercial growth of New York City in the first half of the 19th century, massive though it was, paled in comparison to the population growth. From 1820 to 1860, numbers soared from 123,000 to 813,000, an explosion due in large part to poor economic conditions in Europe. Irish and Germans, in particular, flooded the city. About half of these immigrants found jobs as servants, rag-trade workers, cooks, and manual labourers. Others worked as skilled craftsmen, and some opened up their own businesses as tailors, jewellers and bakers.

Immigrant neighbourhoods consisting primarily of Italians or Germans, Scandinavians or Russians, Jews or Irish, began popping up

No matter their origins, all New Yorkers appreciate a green space for an al fresco lunch.

throughout the city. Cramped living conditions, no running water, poor sanitation, disease and crime were constant problems. On the other hand, these ethnic communities doubled as small support groups, making loans to each other and opening businesses in partnerships, maintaining customs and practising their religions together, holding festivals in the streets. Social networks that still exist eased the transition of the immigrants into their new homes.

In a show of solidarity and mutual support, immigrants began to form labour unions. Allegiances that transcended nationality and ethnicity were established, with the hope of improving the lives of all the immigrant labourers: Irish and Germans formed the Central Labor Union in 1882 to press for better wages. A group of Jewish and Italian women founded the International Ladies Garment Union in order to secure a 52-hour working week, overtime pay and legal holidays. And Sydney Hillman, a Russian-born Jew, led the Amalgamated Clothing Workers of America in their fight for unemployment insurance, affordable cooperative housing and the creation of banks tailored to fit the needs of the working class.

Expansion and Restriction

As conditions and wages improved, so too did productivity. In 1870, the first railcar was introduced, carrying 400,000 passengers in its first year of operation. In 1877, the American Museum of Natural History was opened, followed shortly by the Metropolitan Museum of Art and the Metropolitan Opera House. The Statue of Liberty was unveiled in 1886, the New York Public Library opened in 1895 and, in 1898, Greater New York was established, encompassing Manhattan, Brooklyn, Queens, the Bronx and Staten Island.

New York continued to grow at the dawn of the 20th century. Between 1892 and 1924, 16 million people passed through Ellis Island, just off the coast of Manhattan. There, in the space of about eight hours, an immigrant was registered, checked for disease or dementia, and sent by ferry to lower Manhattan. Many continued further into the interior of the United States or along the eastern seaboard before settling down, but a third of these immigrants remained in New York. In addition to vast numbers of Germans and Irish, the newcomers included Norwegians, Swedes, Czechoslovakians, Romanians, Russians, Poles, Swedes and Cubans.

These new immigrants were accused of spreading poverty, filth and disease, of stealing jobs and committing crimes. The federal government responded by passing a series of laws to regulate the number of foreigners entering the country. The Chinese and Japanese were barred from entering the US, and criminals, contract labourers or anyone thought to be suffering from insanity or contagious disease were also excluded.

Depression

By 1920, the population of New York and its boroughs had risen to about 5.5 million. Remarkably, 40 per cent of the city's residents were foreign-born. In October 1929, the stock market crashed, closing businesses throughout the city and leaving thousands of New Yorkers unemployed. But Mayor Fiorello La Guardia, the son of an Austrian mother and an Italian father, implemented plans for the construction of bridges and tunnels, schools, parks, hospitals and highways. He also managed to create jobs and improve the infrastructure of the city.

All That Jazz

The stock market crash had a widespread impact. Home to some 200,000 blacks just before the crash, Harlem was an established cultural and economic centre. Black-owned businesses flourished, politicians wielded considerable power, and the cultural scene was hugely influential. La Guardia's initiatives for the rest of the city were not extended to the black community, and without help from city government, Harlem succumbed to poverty and homelessness.

After World War II, New York maintained its reputation as one of the most important commercial centres in the world. But with the opening of the United Nations in 1946, the emergence of the Beat Generation in the 1950s and student activism of the '60s, Manhattan quickly won itself a reputation as a cultural and artistic hot spot. It was said that in 1960, more than two-thirds of the country's better-known artists were living in New York.

The backdrop to modern-day New York remains much as it was in the 19th century. The city has continued to attract people from throughout the world. Africans, Central Americans, Indians, Greeks, Asians, Mexicans, South Americans and West Indians are the newest and best-represented immigrants. New York's ethnic communities still thrive, doubling as a welcoming committee for the new arrivals and simultaneously adding a dimension to New York that is invaluable and irreplaceable.

Ground Zero and Beyond

On September 11, 2001, two hijacked passenger aircraft slammed into the Twin Towers of the World Trade Center in downtown Manhattan, killing almost 3,000 people of many nationalities that worked in the buildings. The financial district and most of downtown Manhattan were paralyzed for weeks as the devastation at Ground Zero, as the site was soon called, was evacuated and the clean-up began.

Repercussions of the attack spread worldwide, as President Bush sought retribution by declaring a war against terrorism. The entire nation felt the anxiety and terror that New York had experienced first hand. For a brief moment in spring, 2002, two columns of light beamed into the sky as a memorial to the lives that were lost. Authorities continue to discuss what to do with the now empty site, while the resilient New Yorkers piece together their shattered self-confidence.

Sightseeing

 New York consists of five boroughs—Brooklyn, the Bronx, Queens, Staten Island and Manhattan. But for millions of visitors, New York is the island of Manhattan. At the heart of the city, 21 km (13 miles) long and 3 km (2 miles) wide, Manhattan encompasses just about everything you'll want to see and experience in the Big Apple. Our sightseeing section slices it up into manageable bite-size chunks:

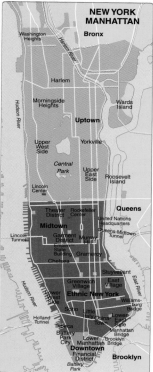

14 ▶ **Downtown**:
The southern tip of Manhattan up to Brooklyn Bridge: Lower Manhattan, the Financial District, Battery Park, Ellis Island

20 ▶ **Ethnic New York**:
Up to 23rd St.: Chinatown, Little Italy, Soho, Greenwich Village

27 ▶ **Midtown**:
34th St to 59th St (East and West): Theater District

35 ▶ **Uptown**:
Upper East Side, Central Park, Upper West Side, Morningside Heights and Harlem

46 ▶ **Other Boroughs**:
Bronx, Queens, Brooklyn and Staten Island

DOWNTOWN

Skyscraper National Park: that's novelist Kurt Vonnegut's apt term for New York. Whereas other cities grew outwards, New York grew up. And up, and up. While there are plenty of beautiful landmarks that don't shoot a thousand feet into the air, the skyscrapers are the true architectural wonders in New York.

City Hall B 7

⋮ Broadway and Chambers St
⋮ Subway: 4, 5, 6, N or R to City Hall
⋮ Tel. (212) 788-6865

Begun in 1803, the headquarters of the city government took eight years to complete. A yellow fever epidemic was blamed for the delay, but a dispute over wages contributed heavily to the hold up. In Federal style (inspired by English neoclassicism), the building is understated, elegant and finely detailed. The security guards will let you enter if you tell them that you want to look around. The domed rotunda in the lobby, the Governor's Room and the Blue Room (where the mayor holds press conferences) are big draws.

References correspond to the fold-out map at the end of the guide.

Woolworth Building B 7

⋮ 233 Broadway opposite
⋮ City Hall Park
⋮ Subway: 4, 5, 6, N or R to City Hall

By 1913, F.W. Woolworth, the retailer who introduced the idea of bringing products out of the warehouse and displaying them on shelves so that customers could see and touch them, had amassed a fortune big enough to pay $13,500,000 in cash for the construction of this building. Nicknamed "the Cathedral of Commerce", it was the tallest in the world at 241 m (792 ft). Take a look at the figures of labourers carved over the front doors and the masks on the façade near the second floor that represent the world's civilizations: Asia, Africa, Europe and America. Then pop inside for a closer look at the legacy of Woolworth's love affair with capitalism. In the hallway near the Broadway side of the building are statues of Mr Woolworth holding a giant nickel, a banker studying trades on Wall St and another gentleman trying to rent out space.

Wall Street A 7

⋮ Subway: 4 or 5 to Wall St

In the middle of the 17th century, a wooden wall was erected in hopes of protecting New Amsterdam's settlers from Indian attacks. That wall is remembered in Wall Street, a rather humble stretch of asphalt between Broadway and the East River, and the catch phrase for one of the busiest financial centres in the world. Not a neighbourhood in the conventional sense of the word, the area is dominated by skyscrapers and office buildings. With few residents, things get quiet at night. But during the day, every nook and cranny in Wall Street is buzzing as money changes hands.

Fraunces Tavern Museum A 8
Subway: 4 or 5 to Wall St
54 Pearl St (at Broad St.)
Tel. (212) 425-1778

This 18th-century tavern has been substantially rebuilt since it was the haunt of George Washington and the Sons of Liberty. It is now a small museum of American History. The Long Room, where Washington made his farewell address to his Revolutionary War officers, is one of the several period rooms on display.

Trinity Church A 7
Broadway and Wall St
Subway: 4 or 5 to Wall St
This Gothic-style church—with its flying buttresses, stained-glass windows and huge bronze doors—looks oddly out of place in the bustling financial district.

GROUND ZERO A 7

The World Trade Center was a complex of several office buildings located in Manhattan's Financial District, housing over 1,200 businesses, banks and government offices. The most famous structures in the complex were the Twin Towers, the tallest in the city at 411 m (1,350 ft). They visually dominated the lower Manhattan skyline with their imposing spires. On September 11, 2001, the world watched with horror and disbelief as two hijacked commercial airplanes crashed into and destroyed both towers, killing everybody aboard both planes and claiming thousands of lives in both of the 100-storey buildings.

Since September 11, the World Trade Center has been referred to as Ground Zero. The enormous clean-up operation is still in progress, and much of the immediate neighbourhood remains ravaged, including the subway lines that once passed underneath the buildings. Viewing platforms have been installed on Fulton St so that visitors may pay their respects to the people who lost their lives. Subway 2, 3, 4 or 5 to Fulton St. Tickets for the viewing platforms are distributed (free of charge) at South Street Seaport, Pier 17.

Constructed in 1846, the church became so dirty over the course of the next century and a half that it was assumed to be black. When the exterior was cleaned in 1991, everyone was stunned to see that the church was actually a rosy pink sandstone.

In the spooky graveyard on the north side of the church, the oldest gravestone is that of Richard Churcher, who died in 1681, aged five. Alexander Hamilton, the first Secretary of the Treasury, is also buried here.

New York Stock Exchange A 7

- Tickets at 20 Board St
- Subway: 4 or 5 to Wall St
- Weekdays 9 a.m.–4.30 p.m.
- Tel. (212) 656-5165

This surprisingly small neoclassical building plays a tremendously important role in the city, both symbolically and practically. When the stock market thrives, so too does New York's reputation as the commercial hub of the US. There's a Visitor's Center on the third floor, where you can look over some informative exhibits on how the market works, and watch the hustle and bustle on the trading floor below. Try to get there before 4 p.m., when the brokers and traders close shop for the day.

Federal Hall National Memorial A 7

- 26 Wall St
- Subway: 4 or 5 to Wall St
- Mon–Fri 10 a.m.–5 p.m.
- Tel. (212) 825 6888

It was here in 1789, on the steps of the Federal Hall, that George Washington was sworn in as the first president of the United States. The building has had many lives since then: it served as City Hall at the close of the 18th century, was then demolished and rebuilt as a US Customs House in 1842, and is now a museum, boasting some fine exhibitions on the history of New York.

South Street Seaport Museum B 7–8

- 207 Water St
- (tickets at 171 John St.)
- Subway: 2, 3, 4, 5, J, M or Z to Fulton St.;
- A or C to Broadway/ Nassau
- April–Sept., Fri–Wed 10 a.m.– 6 p.m., Thurs to 8 p.m.;
- Oct.–March, Wed–Mon 10 a.m.–5 p.m.
- Tel. (212) 748-8600

This isn't so much a museum as an outdoor exhibition, celebrating New York's deep cultural and historical roots in maritime trading. Cobbled streets line the large area in the heart of New York's 19th-century port district, on the shore of the East River. There are indoor exhibits highlighting the history of shipping in New York, as well as galleries featuring dramatic seascape paintings. The real attraction, however, is the fleet of historic ships lined up along the museum's dock, the largest collection of this kind in the world.

Brooklyn Bridge B 7–8

Considered by many to be the most beautiful bridge in the whole country, it connects Brooklyn to Manhattan. Construction was beset by a series of tragedies. Designer John Roebling was killed in a boating accident. His son Washington Roebling then began supervising construction but was crippled in a diving accident. Twenty people lost their lives while working on the bridge, and twelve pedestrians were trampled to death on the walkway just a week after the bridge opened. Its death-toll notwithstanding, the Brooklyn Bridge remains one of the most beloved structures in the city.

The massive anchorages supporting the bridge are hollow and, for a time, the one nearest to Manhattan was used as a cellar for storing wine.

Make sure to take in the views from the pedestrian promenade.

Vietnam Veterans Memorial A 8

Coenties Slip,
between Water and South Sts
Subway: 4 or 5 to Bowling Green

Completed in 1985, this moving memorial includes sections from soldier's letters, excerpts from speeches and reporters' dispatches from the Vietnam War—all etched into a greenish glass-brick wall. The memorial can be found in the Vietnam Veterans Plaza.

Battery Park A 8

Southern tip of Manhattan
Subway: 4 or 5 to Bowling Green

If you're on your way to Ellis Island or the Statue of Liberty, you'll probably be heading through Battery Park, the area where the original European settlers established their colony. The present-day view from the park, however, is much different from that of the 17th century. Looking south, you can see the graceful lines of the Verrazano Bridge, the docks of New Jersey, Staten Island, the Statue of Liberty and Ellis Island. Behind you loom the skyscrapers of the financial district. The Netherlands Memorial is near the park entrance, The Immigrants near Castle Clinton, and the East Coast Memorial on the water's edge, just east of the castle.

National Museum of the American Indian A 8

- Heye Center
- 1 Bowling Green (between Whitehall and State Sts)
- Subway: 4 or 5 to Bowling Green
- Daily 10 a.m.–5 p.m., Thurs to 8 p.m.
- Tel. (212) 668-6624

Located in the former US Customs House, this museum displays an unsurpassed collection of Native American artefacts assembled by George Gustave Heye. Highlights are feathered headdresses, weapons and silver jewellery. The restored murals in the rotunda are outstanding.

Castle Clinton A 8

- Battery Park
- Subway: 9, N or R to Whitehall St/South Ferry;
- 4 or 5 to Bowling Green
- Tours hourly, 10.35 a.m.–3.35 p.m. daily
- Tel. (212) 269-5755

The chances are good that at some point in your stay you'll find yourself inside the 2.5-m-thick (8-ft) stone walls of this restored 19th-century fortress buying tickets for the ferry ride to Ellis Island. The castle was built in 1807, during the period leading to the War of 1812, in order to protect New York from encroaching British ships.

Ellis Island Immigration Museum

- Ellis Island, off the southern tip of Manhattan
- Mon–Sun 9.30 a.m.–5 p.m., longer in summer
- Tel. (212) 269-5755 for ferry information

From Battery Park, catch a ferry to the museum and on the way enjoy a great view of the city skyline and the Statue of Liberty. The museum was opened in 1990, after extensive renovations to the original building that had assessed more than 12 million immigrants between 1892 and 1954. It features some truly moving displays spread over three floors, and you will need at least three hours to do it justice.

Treasures from Home is an exhibit of family heirlooms and photographs carried by the immigrants on their journey to America, while Peak Immigration Years shows photographs, letters, clothing and news stories, all documenting the joys, sorrows, triumphs and challenges faced by the immigrants in their new homes. One of the most spectacular exhibits is the circular American Immigrant Wall of Honor just outside the museum, on which the names of more than 420,000 immigrants are inscribed.

Statue of Liberty

Liberty Island
Subway: 9, N or R to Whitehall
St/South Ferry;
4 or 5 to Bowling Green
Ferry information:
Tel. (212) 269-5755
Frequent ferry departures from
Battery Park

A symbol of freedom and opportunity, the Statue of Liberty is America's most enduring icon. The massive sculpture, standing more than 92 m (300 ft) above New York Harbor, was designed and built by the French sculptor Frédéric Auguste Bartholdi. Completed in Paris in 1884, the statue was dismantled, shipped and presented as a gift from the French people to the United States two years later. Liberty is portrayed wresting her feet free of iron shackles; her right hand raises a torch aloft, her left holds a tablet representing the Declaration of Independence. To celebrate its centenary, the statue underwent a $150 million facelift. Since the terrorist attacks of September 11, the statue has been closed to visitors. You can take the ferry to Liberty Island and view the "Lady" up close but you can not go inside the monument.

CITY TOURS

A wealth of companies in Manhattan offer tours of the city, by bus, helicopter or boat. Whatever the mode of transport, all of them afford an intimate look at New York, often with live narration.

Boat and helicopter tours offer the bonus of a close-up of the Statue of Liberty and Ellis Island.

– Circle Line Cruise: Pier 83, W. 42nd St and 12th Ave; Tel. (212) 563-3200
– Spirit Cruise: Pier 62, Chelsea Piers, W. 23rd St.; Tel. (212) 727-2789
– The Spirit of New York: Pier 62, W. 23rd St and 12th Ave,
  Tel. (212) 742-7278
– Island Helicopter Sightseeing: E. 34th St and East River; Tel. (212) 683-4575
– Liberty Helicopter Tours: Midtown: W. 30th St and 12th Ave, Tel. (212) 465-
  8905 or 967-6464; downtown: Pier 6 at the East River, between South
  Street Seaport and Battery Park, Tel. (212) 465-8905 or (212) 967-6464.
Buses reach the most interesting parts of town and let you hop off and on.
– Gray Line New York: 900 Eighth Ave, between 53rd and 54th Sts,
  Tel. (212) 397-2600
– New York Visions: Broadway and W. 53rd St., Tel. (212) 391-0900
– New York Doubledecker Tours: Empire State Building, 34th St and Fifth
  Ave, Tel. (212) 967-6008

ETHNIC NEW YORK

During your visit, you'll no doubt hear people mentioning the names of various neighbourhoods: SoHo, Little Italy, Chinatown, the Upper West Side, TriBeCa, the West Village, and so on. These exciting districts each have their own special character, and often you will leave one world and enter another just by crossing the street. It's important to remember that, in terms of space, Manhattan is not a big city. In fact, you can walk from the east end of the island to the west in half an hour, making the area one of the best parts of New York to see on foot. So put on your walking shoes and be on your way!

Chinatown B–C 6–7

⋮ Stretches north to Delancey St., south to Worth St., east to Allen St and west to Broadway
⋮ Subway: N, R, M, J or 6 to Canal St

Until 1965, there was a strict quota on the number of Chinese allowed entry to the US. But once the restriction was lifted, Chinatown began to expand. It has grown from a small neighbourhood of seven blocks and some 20,000 people into the most populous Chinese community in the western hemisphere, with four times as many residents. Prepare yourself for the inescapable and seductive aroma of Asian cuisine, winding, congested streets, throngs of people, and vendors hawking everything from trinkets and odd bits of clothing to contraband fireworks and fresh vegetables and meat. This is an enticing neighbourhood for bargain shopping and good restaurants. Chinatown, Little Italy and the East Village are known collectively as the Lower East Side.

Museum of the Chinese Americans B 7

⋮ 70 Mulberry St (at Bayard St.)
⋮ Subway: N, R, M, J or 6 to Canal St
⋮ Tues–Sat noon–5 p.m.
⋮ Tel. (212) 619–4785

The only museum documenting the history of Chinese Americans, it is located on the second floor of a century-old school building.

First Shearith Israel Graveyard B 7

⋮ 55–57 St James Place (between Oliver and James Sts)
⋮ Subway: N, R, M, J or 6 to Canal St

On the edge of Chinatown, this small cemetery is the oldest surviving graveyard for the Jewish congregation in North America. The oldest tombstone dates from 1683.

Church of the Transfiguration B 7
- 25 Mott St
- Subway: N, R, M, J or 6 to Canal St
- Tel. (212) 962-5157

This beautiful 200-year-old church is unique for its predominantly Chinese Catholic congregation. The interior is lovingly decorated.

Little Italy B–C 6
- Mulberry and Broome Sts
- Subway: B, D or Q to Grand St

Little Italy has shrunk since the 1920s, when it was bordered by Houston, Canal St., the Bowery and Broadway, and virtually all its residents, or their ancestors, had immigrated from Italy. Today, most of the neighbourhood's bakeries, restaurants and vendors are located on just two streets, and everything else has been swallowed up by Chinatown. Size notwithstanding, this is one of the best places in the city for genuine Italian fare, and the neighbourhood in itself is practically a museum. The former Umberto's Clamhouse, on the corner of Hester and Mulberry, is where the infamous gangster Joey Gallo was shot down in the middle of a plate of scungilli. Martin Scorsese based much of his film *Goodfellas* on his exposure to mobsters during his childhood in Little Italy.

Don't miss the cafés and pastry shops along Broome and Mulberry streets.

New York Police Headquarters B 6
- 240 Centre St
- (between Broome and Grand)
- Subway: B, D or Q to Grand St

This elegant, domed Edwardian baroque building was completed in 1909 as City Police Headquarters. It was converted into luxury apartments in 1988.

Old St Patrick's Cathedral C 6
- Prince St (at Mulberry St.)
- Subway: 6 to Spring St

The cathedral was founded in 1809 by Irish immigrants and was the parish church until 1879 when the new St Patrick's on Fifth Ave eclipsed it. The old cathedral has achieved fame as the childhood parish of Martin Scorsese and as the backdrop in two of Francis Ford Coppola's "Godfather" films.

Children's Museum of the Arts B 6
- 118 Mercer between Prince and Spring Sts
- Subway: 6 to Spring St
- Tues and Thurs 10 a.m.–11.30 a.m.;
- Wed and Fri 1 p.m.–5 p.m.
- Tel. (212) 941-9198

Small-town atmosphere in a corner of Greenwich Village.

Most kids arrive at the Children's Museum with little or no notion of art, and leave it a budding Picasso or Georgia O'Keeffe. Children aged 1 to 10 can hide away in a corner with a colouring book, toss multi-coloured balls in the Monet Ball Pond, or participate in one of the organized art activities.

TriBeCa A–B 6

⋮ Bordered by Canal St., Broadway,
⋮ Barclay and the Hudson River.
⋮ Subway: 1 or 9 to Canal St

An abbreviated place-name, meaning "Triangle Below Canal", TriBeCa occupies a roughly trapezoidal area. If you'd really like to live in SoHo but your paintings aren't selling for $200,000 apiece, this is where you'd look for a flat and expect to find the same upper-class bohemian atmosphere, elegant cast-iron buildings and trendy boutiques and galleries.

Duane Park B 7

⋮ Hudson and Duane Sts
⋮ Subway: 1, 2, 3 or 9
⋮ to Chambers St

TriBeCa's green space, Duane Park is a trinagular patch of land that was a formal garden in the early 1880s.

Washington Market Park A 6
- Greenwich and Chambers Sts
- Subway: 1, 2, 3 or 9
- to Chambers St

A green space tucked into a busy corner.

SoHo B 6
- Bordered by Houston St., Canal St., Crosby St., and Sixth Ave
- Subway: C or E to Spring St
- N or R to Prince St

SoHo is the truncated name for the area just "South of Houston". Throughout the 19th century, SoHo was home to New York's finest hotels, theatres and department stores. But by the 1950s many of the businesses had moved uptown, leaving empty warehouses and loft spaces in their wake. In the 1960s, struggling artists, actors and writers got wind of the bargain rents and moved to the neighbourhood in droves. Today movie stars and fashion models are among those who frequent its galleries, restaurants, cafés and boutiques. This is the place to stargaze while you sip a $5 cappuccino. The SoHo area has the biggest concentration of cast-iron buildings in New York; don't miss those along Greene St, between nos. 8 and 24, the Roosevelt Building, 478–482 Broadway and the Haughwout Store, 488–492 Broadway.

Guggenheim Museum SoHo B 6
- 575 Broadway at Prince St
- Subway: N or R to Prince St
- Tel. (212) 423-3500 for hours

Look into the Guggenheim's SoHo branch, particularly if you're interested in photographer Robert Mapplethorpe's work.

New York City Fire Museum B 6
- 278 Spring St
- Subway: 1 or 9 to Canal St
- Tel. (212) 691-1303

Located in a 1904 firehouse, the museum displays historic firefighting equipment and traces the history of New York's bravest heroes from the 1600s to the present day.

Greenwich Village B–E 5–6
- Bounded by 14th St., Houston St., the Hudson River and the East River.
- Subway: A, B, C, D, E or F to West 4th St./Washington Square

The Village is a hotbed of political activism, the foundation of the gay rights movement, and home to some of the country's most talented artists, musicians, actors and writers. For a century and a half, it has occupied an almost mythological position in American traditions. The area's radical politics and trendy arts and music scene are due in large part to the endless stream of young students at New York University, the country's largest private university. The elegant brick townhouses, a labyrinth of narrow streets that wind their way through the neighbourhood with no apparent rhyme or reason, quaint antique stores, alternative bookstores and dimly lit bars that serve rare scotches and dark beers are only a few of the reasons tourists and natives alike flock here.

Don't miss Balducci's gourmet food store at Sixth Ave and 9th St.; it has been specializing in takeaway Italian dishes since 1948.

Church of the Ascension C 5
Fifth Ave at 10th St
Subway: N or R to 8th St
Tel. (212) 254-8620
Completed in 1841, this Gothic Revival style brownstone structure was the first church completed on Fifth Ave, then an unpaved track. The beautiful interior is famous for its John LaFarge mural and extensive stained-glass windows.

Jefferson Market Library C 5
Sixth Ave and 10th St
Subway: N or R to 8th St
An eyeful of bright red stone, ornate pinnacles, towers and

carvings, this building is hard to miss. It houses a branch of the New York Public Library but was originally built in 1877 as a courthouse.

Washington Square C 5
At foot of Fifth Ave, at 4th St
Subway: A, B, C, D, E, F or Q to West 4th St./Washington Square
For ad hoc performance art and a glimpse at the student culture that is so much a part of Greenwich Village, you can't top Washington Square Park. It was nothing but a marsh till the end of the 18th century and also served as a cemetery, site of the hangman's gallows and military parade ground. Bordered to the south by New York University's academic buildings, it doubles as a lunch spot and social area for NYU students and neighbourhood tenants. Grass is something of a commodity here, but the designers made sure to include rows of benches along the paths. You will probably see a comedy routine or an acrobatic show in progress.

If you like chess, stroll over to the southwest corner of the park and test your wits against a local. Washington Arch, at the northern end, was erected in 1892 in honour of the 100th anniversary of George Washington's inauguration as first president of the US. Though the arch was originally built of wood, it proved so popular that it was restructured in marble. It marks the end of Fifth Ave and the beginning of Greenwich Village.

Grace Church C 5
: 802 Broadway (at 10th St.)
: Subway: N or R to 8th St
This Gothic-style Episcopalian church, built in 1846, was designed by James Renwick, later the architect of St Patrick's Cathedral. Long a center for the evangelical Low Church movement, Grace Church has operated overseas missions and a shelter for the homeless.

East Village
: Bordered by the East River to the Bowery, from 14th St to Houston St
: Subway: 6 to Astor Place
Since it stopped being Peter Stuyvesant's *bouwerie* (Dutch for farm) and grew up into a neighbourhood, the East Village has been the city's place for bold bohemian statements. It has not completely lost the rough edge it acquired in the 1960s when radicals, hippies, musicians and artists flocked here after being priced out of Greenwich Village. Now a melting pot of various ethnic groups, the East Village remains full of life and flavour.

Tompkins Square D 6
: Bordered by Aves. A and B and 7th and 10th Sts
: Subway: 6 to Astor Place
This is the best place in New York for a look at the city's still-thriving immigrant culture. Elderly Russians, Ukrainians and Poles share the park with the younger blacks and Hispanics. You'll generally find the former sitting on the benches or playing draughts near the south side of the park, while the latter play basketball on the north side courts. In the centre of the park is a statue of two children looking at a steamboat, a memorial to the 1,200 women and children—most of them German immigrants from this neighbourhood—who were killed in a terrible ferry accident on the East River in 1904. The park is perfectly safe during the day, but be watchful if you venture into the grounds after sunset.

Merchant's House Museum C 6
: 29 East 4th St
: (between Lafayette and Bowery)
: Subway: 6 to Astor Place
: Tel. (212) 777-1089
This small town house museum gives an accurate picture of

gracious living in the 19th century, with its original furnishings and decor.

St Mark's Church in the Bowery C 5
- 131 East 19th St
- (between Second and Third aves.)
- Subway: 6 to Astor Place
- Tel. (212) 674-6377

The church sits on land that was once the farm of New Amsterdam's Governor Peter Stuyvesant (he and his wife are buried under the church). Completed in 1799, it is the city's second-oldest church, after St Paul's. The interior has been restructured into a versatile performance space after a devastating fire in 1978.

Chelsea B–C 4
- Bounded by the Hudson River, Fifth Ave, 14th and 23rd Sts
- Subway: A, C or E to 23rd St

As real estate prices and rents skyrocketed in the West Village, young professionals began migrating north to Chelsea (named by an English officer after the district in London). These new (and wealthier) residents mixed with the largely immigrant population, and retailers soon saw the potential. Stores were built in renovated factories, restaurants took the place of corner delis and warehouses were transformed into nightclubs. Chelsea's weekend flea-markets, lively dance clubs and cavernous department stores on Sixth Ave are its main attractions. At 222 West 23rd Street, the brownstone Chelsea Hotel has long been a favourite with writers and artists.

Union Square Greenmarket C 5
- East 17th St and Broadway
- Subway. L, N, Q, R, W, 4, 5 or 6 to 14th Street
- Tel. (212) 477-3220
- Mon, Wed, Fri, Sat 7 a.m.–6 p.m.

The city's premier greenmarket is held al fresco year round in Union Square, featuring the finest produce, organics, baked goods, exotic flowers and more. Everything is fresh, the prices are good and the people friendly.

Flatiron Building C 4
- 175 Fifth Ave,
- between 22nd and 23rd Sts
- Subway: N, R, F or 6 to 23rd St

Originally called the Fuller Building, after its developer, this is another distinctive New York City structure. The 90-m (300-ft) Flatiron Building was completed in 1902 and figured, for a time, as the tallest building in the world. The rounded corner at the northern end is only 2 m (6 ft) across.

MIDTOWN

From the Hudson River to the East River, from 34th to 59th Sts, Midtown (East and West) is the shopping, dining, theatre-going, people-watching heart of New York. You can find almost anything in Midtown if you don't mind the hustle and bustle of the city's busiest intersections.

Madison Square Garden C 4

- 2 Penn Plaza
- (at 33rd St and Seventh Ave)
- Subway: A, C, E, 1, 2, 3 or 9 to 34th St
- Tel (212) 621-6600

The premier sports arena in the city, whether you are a Knicks or Rangers fan. Also a favourite concert venue and home of the New York Horse Show. Visitors may take a tour of the 20,000-seat arena.

Empire State Building D 4

- 350 Fifth Ave at 34th St
- Subway: N, R, B, D, F or Q to Herald Square/34th St
- Daily 9.30 a.m.–11.30 p.m.
- Tel. (212) 736-3100, or (212) 279-9777 for New York Skyride

The Empire State Building remains one of the city's most beloved landmarks. Built in 1931, the 380-m (1,250-ft) structure (not counting the TV tower) reigned as the world's tallest building until the 1970s. It is the stuff of legends. In 1933, the building saw its first suicide when one Erma Eberhardt leapt to her death. Later that year, King Kong made his way to the top on film screens, only to face a squadron of planes and fall from the building as dramatically as Eberhardt. One foggy day in July 1945, a real Army B-25 crashed into the 79th floor, killing 14 people, and in 1986 a couple of British tourists parachuted from the 86th floor. Today, some 2.5 million visitors make their way up the building for the views from the observation decks on the 86th and 102nd floors, where you can see all Manhattan and the four outer boroughs. Don't miss the New York Skyride on the second floor, a new flight-simulator that takes you on an airborne tour of the city.

United Nations E 4

- First Ave at 46th St
- Subway: 4, 5, 6, 7 or S to Grand Central Terminal/42nd St
- Tours daily 9.15 a.m.–4.45 p.m. (Jan–Feb, weekdays only)
- Tel. (212) 963-7713

Once you set foot in the United Nations, you are technically no longer in New York. Nor in the US, for that matter. The entire area between 42nd and 48th Sts on York Ave is international territory. There's much to be seen at the UN: a row of flags representing each member nation, the Secretariat and General Assembly buildings, the Dag Hammarskjold Library (named after the UN Secretary-General killed in 1961 during a peace mission to Zaire) and the Conference Building. Join one of the tours leaving every 30 min from the General Assembly lobby. You can enjoy the wonderful rose garden without the help of a tour guide.

Chrysler Building E 4

405 Lexington Ave, between 42nd and 43rd Sts
Subway: 4, 5, 6, 7 or S to 42nd St

Throughout the first half of the 20th century, a feverish competition raged among architects to build the city's tallest structure. In 1929, H. Craig Severance unveiled the 283-m (927-ft) Bank of Manhattan and declared that the contest was over. But when the Chrysler Building's steel spire was put in place, for a total height of 319 m (1,048 ft), the building eclipsed not only Severance's structure, but Paris's Eiffel Tower as well. Do not miss the beautifully

appointed lobby. And you can't help but admire the stainless steel exterior.

Grand Central Terminal D 3-4

East 42nd St at Park Ave
Subway: 4, 5, 6, 7 or S to Grand Central Terminal/42nd St
Tours every Wed at 12.30 p.m.
Tel. (212) 935-3960

Not everyone who works in Manhattan lives there, and the vast majority of those who commute go through Grand Central Terminal. What has so intrigued visitors and natives alike is that engineers managed to bring a bustling railway system into the heart of one of the busiest cities in the world—and do it silently and invisibly through tunnels. It is crowned by a beautiful Beaux Arts structure. The better part of the station is taken up by one vast room—the main concourse—through which 150,000 passengers pass daily. The ceiling—twelve stories up—displays the Zodiac constellation. For some time it was obscured by a heavy accumulation of grime, but in 1997 a full restoration and cleaning was completed. Three intricate sculptures, a massive clock and a

The Chrysler Building clad in gleaming stainless steel.

row of arched windows grace the terminal's southern facade. The best spot to appreciate the intricate beauty of this building is from the corner of 39th St and Park Avenue.

New York City Library D 3

Fifth Ave, between 40th and 42nd Sts

Subway: 4, 5, 6, 7, B, D, F, Q or S to 42nd St

Mon, Thurs–Sat 10 a.m.–6 p.m.; Tues–Wed, 11 a.m.–7.30 p.m.

Tel. (212) 930-0800

One of the best places to observe this city in perpetual motion is on the steps of the main branch of the New York Public Library. Take a seat between the two marble lions dubbed "Patience" and "Fortitude" and watch the theatre of Manhattan unfold. As to the library itself, possessing 9 million volumes, it is widely renowned as one of the pre-eminent research facilities in the world. If you want to see the cavernous main reading room, the periodical room, the library's art gallery and its beautiful Beaux Arts interior, ask at the information desk for a schedule of the free one-hour tours given by the library staff.

Bryant Park D 3

Bordered by 42nd and 40th Sts, between Fifth and Sixth Aves.

Subway: B, D, F or Q to 42nd St

Named after poet William Cullen Bryant, this midtown park is popular with visitors and locals alike. It's a perfect place to enjoy an outdoor lunch with the throngs of business people that have turned Bryant Park into a midday eatery. There's a restaurant and café and, though you wouldn't guess it, the park sits over a vast tomb that houses part of New York Public Library's extensive collections.

Intrepid Sea-Air-Space Museum B–C 2

Pier 86 at Hudson River, 46th St and 12th Ave

Subway: Any 42nd St stop, plus crosstown bus

May–Sept., Mon–Sat 10 a.m.– 5 p.m., Sun to 6 p.m.; Oct.–April, Wed–Sun 10 a.m.–5 p.m.

Last admissions one hour before closing.

Tel. (212) 245-0072

Commissioned in 1942, this massive aircraft carrier, with a crew of 3,000, served in World War II, the Korean and Vietnam wars. Renovated in 1982, the *Intrepid* now serves as a museum.

If you're interested in seeing the innards of a warship, inspecting the cockpit of the world's fastest jet (the spyplane Blackbird on deck), or exploring the interior of a submarine docked nearby, this is an exciting place to do it. It's a must for children.

Times Square D 3

Subway: N, R, 1, 2, 3 or 9 to 42nd St

Not too long ago, Times Square (named after the *New York Times,* which was based for 20 years in the tower at no. 1) was the domain of panhandlers, pickpockets and prostitutes, but the derelicts have now moved on and Mickey Mouse has taken it by storm. In the late 1980s, the city decided to repair the crumbling buildings, clean up the streets, tighten security and bring in new storefronts. As they lacked the requisite funds, Disney offered to help revamp the area. Mickey's big black nose has put grins on the faces of local politicians and the throngs of tourists that visit the area every year, though some locals are worried about the effects of commercialization. Still, there are few places as exciting and overwhelming as Times Square. The glittering neon signs are as impressive as ever and, if you're looking for tickets to Broadway shows, souvenirs, toys for the kids or CDs to take home, this is the place to go. Peep into the Algonquin Hotel at 59 W. 44th St.

Rockefeller Center D 3

Fifth to Seventh Aves. and 47th to 52nd Sts
Subway: N to 49th St.; B, D, F or Q to 47th/50th Sts/Rockefeller Center

In the heart of midtown is a giant complex of office buildings, theatres and underground pedestrian passageways and shops, constructed in the 1930s and collectively known as Rockefeller Center. Almost 300,000 people come to the Center every day, either to work or just to visit. The main attractions are the Channel Gardens (just off Fifth Ave between 49th and 50th Sts), so called because the promenade separates the British Empire Building from the Maison Française. There's a huge gilded bronze statue of Prometheus by Paul Manship at the western end of the promenade, in the sunken Lower Plaza that serves as an outdoor café during the summer and an ice-skating rink throughout the winter. The furniture and frescoes of Radio City Music Hall (America's largest indoor theatre), are listed as historic monuments; and the Art Deco General Electric Building (home to the NBC television network and, for many years, the site of David Letterman's *Late Night* studio) is also popular.

Christie's New York D 3

Rockefeller Center
20 Rockefeller Plaza at 49th St
Subway: B, D, F or Q
Rockefeller Center
Mon 10 a.m.–7 p.m.; Tues–Sat
10 a.m.–5 p.m.; Sun 1–5 p.m.
Tel. (212) 636-2000

Christie's offers a similar experience to rival Sotheby's. A trip to both houses offers a fascinating view of the world of high-stakes auctioning.

Radio City Music Hall D 3

1260 Avenue of the Americas (at 50th St)
Subway: B, D, F or Q to
Rockefeller Center
Tel. (212) 307-1000

Completed in 1932, Radio City Music Hall is the city's most notable Art Deco masterpiece. The vast auditorium and stage is home to the everlasting Rockettes, precision dancers, and their fabulous holiday and seasonal theatrical dance entertainments. Don't miss the Old Faithful of Manhattan!

St Patrick's Cathedral D–E 3

Fifth Ave at 50th St
Subway: B, D, F or Q to 47th/50th Sts/Rockefeller Center;
E, F, to 53rd St.; 6 to 51st St
Tel. (212) 753-2261

SHOPPING IN MIDTOWN

Whatever you want, you can find it in New York. Inevitably, you'll spot a bargain price on an antique clock, an oriental rug, a rocking chair or set of dishes. But how are you going to get them home? The sales assistant can advise you about overseas shipping policies.

Keep in mind that nothing is more sacred to Americans than shopping. Accordingly, all the big stores are open seven days a week, well into the evening. Here are the most prestigious shops in Midtown.

– Bloomingdales, 1000 Third Ave (at 59th St.)
– Macy's: 151 West 34th St (34th St at Herald Square)
– Bergdorf Goodman: 754 Fifth Ave (at 58th St)
– Saks Fifth Ave: 611 Fifth Ave (at 49th St)
– Henri Bendel: 712 Fifth Ave (at 56th St)
– Takashimaya: 683 Fifth Ave (at 54th St)
– Tiffany: 57th St and Fifth Ave.
– F.A.O. Schwartz: 767 Fifth Ave (at 59th St)

On 57th St., between Fifth and Madison, you'll find a gaggle of designer fashion and accessory houses to tempt your taste and your credit card: Chanel, Burberry, Hermes to mention but a few.

Home to the Roman Catholic Archdiocese of New York and a symbol of the influence and success of Irish immigrants throughout the US, St Patrick's Cathedral—the largest cathedral in the country—sits elegantly amid the skyscrapers of midtown. The land on which the cathedral is built was originally destined to be a cemetery, but the ground proved far too rocky for burials, so in 1850 Archbishop John Hughes announced his plans to build a cathedral "worthy of God, worthy of the Catholic religion, and an honor to this great city". Construction began in 1859, but because of the Civil War, the cathedral was not completed until 1879. Tours through the Gothic cathedral are available, but it's best to phone in advance for the timetable.

Mary Boone D 3
745 Fifth Ave, 4th Floor
Subway: 4, 5 or 6 to 42nd St
Tues–Fri 10 a.m.–6 p.m.;
Sat to 5 p.m.
Tel. (212) 752-2929

The centre of the red-hot 1980s art market, now working hard at becoming one of the leading galleries of the 3rd millennium, Mary Boone represents the survivors of one age and the newcomers of the next.

Museum of Television and Radio D 3
25 West 52nd St
Subway: E or F to 53rd St
Bus: Downtown via Fifth Ave, uptown via Madison Ave
Tues–Sun noon–6 p.m.;
Thurs to 8 p.m.
Tel. (212) 621-6600

There's a growing school of thought that contemporary American culture owes more to television than literature, theatre and music combined. This museum will convince you it's true. There's an enormous collection of 75,000 recorded radio and television shows dating back to the golden age of television and almost a hundred consoles where, for up to two hours, you can do as the Americans do… watch TV.

American Craft Museum D 3
40 West 53rd St
Subway: 1 to 50th St.;
B to 57th St.; D or E to 53rd St
Bus: Uptown via Madison/Sixth Aves, downtown via Fifth Ave
Tues, Wed, Fri–Sun
10 a.m.–6 p.m.; Thurs to 8 p.m.
Tel. (212) 956-3535

The three levels of galleries in this midtown museum offer exhibitions on contemporary crafts, including works done in ceramic, glass, wood, paper and metal. Some pieces veer sharply towards the experimental, like an outdoor sculpture by Texan Jesus Batista Moroles consisting of a pile of rough or polished granite slabs suggesting… whatever you like to imagine. Good gift shop.

Museum of Modern Art D 3

West 53rd St., between Fifth and Sixth Aves
Closed for renovation until 2005. Collections transferred to temporary location, MoMA QNS, 33 St at Queens Blvd, Long Island City, Queens
Shuttle bus Saturday and Sunday from West 23rd St.
Subway: 7 (local train) to 33 St Queens
Bus Q60 to Queens Blvd
Mon, Thurs, Sun 10 a.m.–5 p.m., Fri 10 a.m.–7.45 p.m.
Tel. (212) 708-9400

The MoMA's collections, transferred to a blue-painted former factory in Queens, are among the most famous in the world. Even if you spend the entire day here you will see only a fraction of the 100,000 paintings, sculptures, drawings, prints and photographs. Every period of modern art, from Expressionism to Cubism, Futurism to Surrealism is represented. Toulouse-Lautrec's *La Goulue at the Moulin Rouge,* Degas's *At the Milliner's,* Picasso's *Girl Before a Mirror,* Van Gogh's *Les Oliviers,* Matisse's *The Blue Window*—and an extensive showcase of some 5,000 photography prints—make the MoMA a must-see for any fan of modern art.

Trump Tower E 3

Fifth Ave at 56th St
Subway: E or F to 53rd St
Tel. (212) 832-2000

Even if you're not going to buy anything in its pricey shops, you must see the lobby of Trump Tower, flashy flagship of controversial real-estate developer Donald Trump.

PaceWildensteinMacGill E 3

32 East 57th St., 9th Floor
Subway: N or R to Fifth Ave
Tues–Fri 9.30 a.m.–5.30 p.m.;
Sat 10 a.m.–6 p.m.
Tel. (212) 759-7999

With three galleries in New York, one in Los Angeles and another in London, PaceWildensteinMacGill handles the works of the world's best-known contemporary artists. Visit any of the New York galleries for a look at the paintings, photographs, drawings and sculptures of artists such as Alexander Calder, Jean Dubuffet, Henry Moore, Claes Oldenburg, Pablo Picasso, Mark Rothko, Julian Schnabel, Kiki Smith and more.

UPTOWN

The stretch of Manhattan from 59th to 96th Sts, sandwiching Central Park in between. East and West sides have different flavours: see them both then decide if you have a preference.

Central Park D 2–F 1

This 340-ha (843-acre) stretch of paths, ponds, trees and grass is as elemental to New Yorkers as water and air. Transformed from swampy wastelands, it is the fruit of a massive project that began in 1857 and took 20 years to complete. There is no end to the list of things you can do here. You can copy the New Yorkers who flock to the vast Sheep Meadow to throw frisbees and sunbathe, rent a bicycle at the Loeb Boathouse, play tennis on one of the park's 26 clay courts, rollerblade along the 72nd St transverse, visit the zoo, or hop in a horse-drawn carriage at Grand Army Plaza for an elegant tour of the grounds. During the winter, you can slip on a pair of ice skates at Wollman Rink and perfect your pirouette.

For a leisurely tour through the park, follow this walking route. Start at the **Carousel**, a turn-of-the-century horse carousel in the south of the park. From there, head northwest to the **Sheep Meadow**, a designated "quiet zone" where you can rest your feet and concentrate on your tan.

Northwest of the meadow is **Strawberry Fields**, Yoko Ono's tribute to her husband John Lennon, in the form of an English-style garden. Head northeast until you reach **Bow Bridge**, offering a fine view of the city.

Southeast of the bridge, you'll reach the **Bethesda Fountain**, a memorial to the soldiers who died in the Civil War. Northeast of the fountain is **Loeb Boathouse**, where you can rent rowing boats and bicycles, or have a snack at the Boathouse Café. Then you're ready for a walk to splendid **Shakespeare Garden** and the Great Lawn, where New Yorkers come to play softball or picnic. To the north is the city's now-unused Reservoir that New Yorkers jog around.

The **Conservatory Garden**, about a mile north of the Reservoir, remains one of the most beautiful, most tranquil and most secretive niches in the park.

Upper East Side F 1–3
Bordered by 59th St., Fifth Ave, the East River and 96th St
Subway: 4, 5 or 6 to 86th St

A clean, safe and well-to-do rectangle, with a postal code—10021—consistently ranked as the richest in the country. Many of the tycoons and industrialists who made their fortunes in the 19th century and their heirs built their mansions in this neighbourhood: Andrew Carnegie, Henry Frick, Louis Comfort Tiffany and Caroline Astor. Most of the New Yorkers living here today share a reputation for being a bit snobbish, with a tendency to display their wealth in the form of limousines, private dog walkers, fur coats and nannies. Don't miss the Gracie Mansion at East End Ave and 88th St., the Carlyle Hotel at 76th St and Madison Ave, and the luxury boutiques along Lexington and Madison Aves.

Queensboro Bridge F 3

If you're a fan of the intricacies of bridge construction, take a quick detour to 60th St and First Ave, preferably at sunset, for a close-up of the Queenboro Bridge, a painting come to life. The 360-m (1,182-ft) steel span links Queens and Manhattan for the convenience of cars, cyclists and pedestrians. It was completed in 1909, but for some time New Yorkers doubted its strength, largely because another bridge of similar style had collapsed. An engineer is said to have eased people's minds after pointing out the endless stream of birds that perched on the bridge, insisting that by instinct they avoid weak structures when looking for a place to rest.

ANTIQUES

New York's open-air flea markets offer old books, antique cameras, used clothing, jewellery, battered furniture and lots of interesting junk. A couple of them charge a small admission, but it's well worth it. The strategy here is to haggle. If you're not one for streetside bargaining, or you're in search of high-end antiques, try the Manhattan Art and Antiques Center or Place des Antiquaires.

– Annex Antiques Fair and Flea Market: 24th–27th Sts at Sixth Ave, Tel. (212) 243-5343. Open Sat and Sun. Subway: N, R, 4, 5 or 6 to 59th St

– Manhattan Art and Antiques Center: 1050 Second Ave between 55th and 56th Sts, Tel. (212) 355-4400. Subway: N, R, 4, 5 or 6 to 59th St.

– Place des Antiquaires: 125 E. 57th St., Tel. (212) 758-2900. Subway: N or R to Fifth Ave.

– PS 44 Flea Market: Columbus Ave between 76th and 77th Sts, Tel. (212) 947-6302. Open Sun. Subway: 1 or 9 to 79th St.

Frick Collection E 2

- 1 East 70th St
- Subway: 6 to 68th St
- Bus: Uptown via Madison Ave, downtown via Fifth Ave
- Tues–Sat 10 a.m.–6 p.m.; Sun from 1 p.m.
- Tel. (212) 288-0700

The Frick Collection is housed in one of the most elegant mansions on Fifth Ave The collection of European paintings (most of them dating from the Renaissance to the late 19th century) rivals that of any major art museum. Titian's *Man in a Red Cap,* Gainsborough's *Sarah, Lady Innes,* Rembrandt's *Portrait of a Young Artist* and Vermeer's *Mistress and Maid* are only a few of the dozens of masterpieces that Henry Clay Frick, who made his fortune in the steel industry, hung on the walls of his home. There's also a fine collection of antique furniture, drawings, porcelains and a delightful indoor courtyard with a fountain.

Knoedler & Co. E–F 2

- 19 East 70th St
- Subway: 6 to 68th St
- Tues–Fri 9.30 a.m.– 5.30 p.m.; Sat from 10 a.m.
- Tel. (212) 794-0550

Knoedler is America's establishment gallery, one of the oldest in the United States, having celebrated its 150th anniversary. Known for its stable of traditional artists, Knoedler represents Impressionist, American and Old Masters paintings, including Cezanne, Georgia O'Keeffe, and Rembrandt.

Sotheby's F 2

- 1334 York Ave at 72nd St
- Subway: 6 to 68th St
- Mon–Fri 10 a.m.–5 p.m.; Sat 1 p.m.–5 p.m.
- Tel. (212) 606-7000

The oldest auction house in the world is one of the secret finds for the art browser. Sotheby's maintains an almost daily rotation of works of art to be auctioned in its various departments, including art of all kinds, furniture, collectibles, jewellery, fashion and wines.

Whitney Museum of American Art F 2

- 945 Madison Ave at 75th St
- Subway: 6 to 77th St
- Bus: Uptown via Madison Ave, downtown via Fifth Ave
- Wed, Fri–Sun 11 a.m.–6 p.m.; Thurs 1–8 p.m.
- Tel. (212) 570-3676

The eccentric socialite Gertrude Vanderbilt Whitney offered her collection to the Metropolitan Museum of Art in 1929, but they turned her down. With a vast inheritance in hand, she opened her own museum, which today houses the most important assemblage of 20th-century American art in the country. Every notable American artist working during this period is represented in the 8,500-piece permanent collection, including Edward Hopper, Jackson Pollock, Jasper Johns, Georgia O'Keeffe, Roy Lichtenstein and Frank Stella. Restaurant and gift shop.

A second branch of the museum, with a fine collection of sculptures, can be found on 42nd St and Park.

Carl Schurtz Park (off map)

East End Ave at 84th St
Subway: 4, 5 or 6 to 86th St
Tel. (212) 360-1311

Stretching along East River, this park is one of the quietest and offers lovely views of the river and its traffic. It is also the site of Gracie Mansion, the mayor's official residence.

Metropolitan Museum of Art F 1

82nd St and Fifth Ave
Subway: 4, 5 or 6 to 86th St
Bus: Uptown via Madison Ave, downtown via Fifth Ave
Tues–Thurs, Sun
9.30 a.m.–5.15 p.m.;
Fri–Sat to 8.45 p.m.
Tel. (212) 879-5500

"The Met" is truly the gem of all American museums, its works a showcase of artistic excellence throughout the history of mankind. Exhibits of European master painters, Roman and Greek sculptors, Chinese calligraphers, African instrument-makers and Egyptian jewellers make up only a small part of the museum's vast collection. Where do you start? Go to the Information Desk for maps, informational brochures, tour schedules and tape-recorded tours. Some of the exhibitions that have been enthralling visitors since the museum's opening in 1870 include a 14,000-piece collection of arms and armour, featuring swords, helmets and arrowheads.

The American Wing traces the progression of American furniture-making, decorative arts and painting since the 18th century. The medieval art collection spans an amazing 12 centuries and includes a stunning display of rare 15th-century tapestries. The galleries in the 19th-century European Paintings and Sculpture section house works by Goya, Rousseau, Rodin, Manet, Cezanne and Degas. Among the musical instruments are rare violins, the oldest existing piano, a jade flute, sitars and gongs. The Met's gift shop is second to none, with an

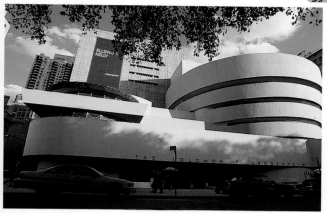

In the Guggenheim the paintings are displayed along a spiralling ramp.

endless selection of posters, slides, jewellery and art books. The roof garden at sunset is a must.

Guggenheim Museum F 1

1071 Fifth Ave at 89th St
Subway: 4, 5 or 6 to 86th St
Bus: Uptown via Madison Ave, downtown via Fifth Ave
Sun–Wed 10 a.m.–6 p.m.;
Fri–Sat to 8 p.m.
Tel. (212) 360-3500

The building itself—designed by Frank Lloyd Wright—has attracted almost as much commentary as the works of art inside. Some critics say the museum looks like a giant toilet, others insist it was Wright's most ingenious design. The exhibition space is shaped liked a spiral, with a curved ramp leading from the ground floor to the top of the building. The idea is to view the works in one continuous line. Van Gogh's *Mountains at Saint Remy,* Cezanne's *Man with Crossed Arms,* Gauguin's *In the Vanilla Grove,* Modigliani's *Nude,* Matisse's *The Italian Woman* and Picasso's *Woman Ironing* are all on permanent display in the Thannhauser Gallery. You can find some great bargains in posters in the museum gift shop.

Cooper-Hewitt Museum F 1

2 East 91st St
Subway: 4, 5 or 6 to 86th St
Bus: Uptown via Madison Ave,
downtown via Fifth Ave
Tues 10 a.m.–9 p.m.;
Wed–Sat to 5 p.m.;
Sun noon–5 p.m.
Tel. (212) 849-8300

Industrialist Andrew Carnegie's
restored 64-room house, built in
1901, is now the National Museum
of Design, housing a collection of
architectural drawings, wood
engravings, porcelain figurines and
a remarkable assortment of
Egyptian, Near Eastern and
Mediterranean fabrics dating back
to the 3rd century. Watch your head
going through the doors: Carnegie
was only 5 ft 2 in tall and he built
the mansion to his own
requirements.

Jewish Museum F 1

1109 Fifth Ave at 92nd St
Subway: 6 to 96th St
Bus: Uptown via Madison Ave,
downtown via Fifth Ave
Mon–Thurs, 9 a.m.–5 p.m.;
Fri to 3 p.m.
Tel. (212) 423-3200

It may not be the most uplifting
stop along Museum Mile, but
it is certainly one of the most
memorable, moving and
educational. There are displays of
Jewish archaeological objects,
some ingenious multi-media
installations and an enormous
collection of drawings, prints and
sculptures.

The Holocaust exhibition on the
third floor is the real attraction.
Two hours spent here will give you
a good idea of how, why and when
the Holocaust happened.

International Center of Photography F 1

1130 Fifth Ave at 94th St
Subway: 6 to 96th St
Bus: Uptown via Madison Ave,
downtown via Fifth Ave
Wed–Sun 11 a.m.–6 p.m.,
Tues to 8 p.m.
Tel. (212) 860-1777 or 860-1778

The Center was founded in 1974
by Cornell Capa to safeguard the
work of his brother Robert, a well-
known photojournalist killed by a
landmine in Vietnam in 1954. It
sponsors about twenty exhibitions
each year. Faithful to Robert Capa's
ideas, the exhibits generally
carry a humanitarian and/or
political message. There are also
retrospectives on master
photographers.

You can spend as much time in the
gift shop as you can in the museum
itself; it contains an extensive
selection of books on photography,
posters and postcards.

Museum of the City of New York (off map)

Fifth Ave and 103rd St
Subway: 6 to 103rd St
Bus: Uptown via Madison Ave, downtown via Fifth Ave
Wed–Sat 10 a.m.–5 p.m.; Sun from 1 p.m.
Tel. (212) 534-1672

This museum depicts the history of New York City. Among the highlights: the Fire Gallery housing fire engines used during the early years of the city fire department; the Toy Gallery showcasing a beautiful collection of antique dollhouses; and the Dutch Gallery, with a fine exhibition detailing 17th-century Dutch history in New York. The collection of photographs by Jacob A. Riis is well worth the admission fee.

El Museo del Barrio (off map)

1230 Fifth Ave at 104th St
Subway: 6 to 103rd St
Bus: Uptown via Madison Ave, downtown via Fifth Ave
Wed–Sun 11 a.m.–5 p.m.; May–Sept., Thurs noon–7 p.m.
Tel. (212) 831-7272

One of the most underrated museums in New York, it all began simply as a display in a school classroom in East Harlem, but now it counts some 8,000 paintings, photographs, sculptures and artefacts in its collection, including the magnificent carvings, "santos de palo". This is the only museum in the nation devoted entirely to the culture of Puerto Rico and Latin America. It radiates an unmistakable feeling of fellowship and warmth that other museums lack and, thanks largely to the ingenuity and hard work of the staff, survives without the massive subsidies enjoyed by the larger institutions in the city.

Upper West Side D–E 1–2

Bounded by the Hudson River, Central Park, 59th St and 125th St
Subway: 1, 2, 3 or 9 to 79th St

East Siders are likely to tell you that West Siders are liberal and unreasonable, and West Siders will retort that East Siders are conservative and greedy. But the dichotomy is outdated: politically, culturally and economically, the Upper West Side is becoming very much like its counterpart to the east, wealthy and conservative. Elegant apartment buildings and townhouses and up-market boutiques line the avenues and cross streets. A landmark: John Lennon lived in the Dakota at Central Park West and 72nd St.; he was murdered on the sidewalk outside in December 1980.

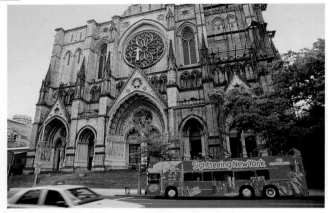

The Gothic cathedral of St John the Divine, still unfinished.

Lincoln Center D 2

- 62nd St and Columbus Ave
- Subway: N or R to 57th St
- Tel. (212) 362-2000

The Lincoln Center for the Performing Arts is awe-inspiring in its comprehensive cultural offerings. Encompassing opera, ballet, theatre, symphony and film in its many and various theatres, it should figure on any visitor's itinerary.

The fountain in the centre of the plaza is great for people-watching and for taking in the grandeur of the setting. Looking at the Center from the front by the fountain, the grand building directly ahead is the Metropolitan Opera. To your right is the Avery Fisher Hall, home of the New York Philharmonic and the city's premier concert location; to your left is the New York State Theater, home of the City Ballet and the City Opera. Although not as grand as its neighbour, the State Theater was designed with dance in mind and has good sightlines and comfortable seats.

One block further uptown, not directly on the plaza, is the Alice Tully Hall, a concert hall for recitals, chamber music, jazz and small-scale opera.

American Museum of Natural History E 1

- 79th St and Central Park West
- Subway: 1, 9 or C to 79th St
- Bus: Uptown via Amsterdam Ave, downtown via Columbus Ave
- Sun–Thurs 10 a.m.–5.45 p.m.; Fri–Sat to 8.45 p.m.
- Tel. (212) 769-5100

The beauties and intricacies of the world's inhabitants—from the first invertebrates to modern man—are underlined in this fascinating museum, which children will love, too. Have a good look at the most minute details of a jellyfish, the hair on the back of a hyena, the teeth of a prehistoric shark and the face paint on an Indian warrior.

If you're in a hurry, at least see the dioramas of wild animals in their natural habitat. You can also admire the famous Star of India—a 563-carat sapphire found 300 years ago in Sri Lanka and the largest known to man. Needless to say, security is pretty strict in this part of the museum.

Tel. (212) 769-5650 for times of shows at the museum's Naturemax Theater, with one of the city's biggest screens.

Riverside Park D 1

- 72nd to 158th St along the Hudson
- Subway: 1, 2, 3 or 9 to 79th St

While you may not be able to cover the entire length of the park, which runs the better part of the western shore of Manhattan, try to stop by the 79th St Boat Basin, a public marina which shelters dozens of houseboats and allows visitors direct access to the Hudson shore and Grant's Tomb (at 122nd St.), the final resting place of Ulysses S. Grant, the Civil War hero and 18th president of the United States.

Morningside Heights (off map)

- Bounded by 125th St., Morningside Park, 110th St and the Hudson River.
- Subway: 1 or 9 to 116th St

A little-known fact about the area is that its prestigious Columbia University (West 116th St., between Amsterdam and Broadway) was built on the grounds of an asylum. Harried students and world-famous intellectuals pop in and out of the bookstores and fast-food sushi bars here. You can see Grant's Tomb at Riverside Drive and 122nd St.

Cathedral of St John the Divine (off map)

- 1047 Amsterdam Ave at 112th St
- Subway: 1 or 9 to 110th St
- Mon–Sun 7 a.m.–7 p.m.
- Tel. (212) 316-7540

Not to be missed! Construction began in 1892, and it's still not finished. The fact that it's almost a century behind schedule seems to add to the legend of this massive structure, which, one day, will be the world's largest Gothic cathedral. At every stage of its building, the limestone and granite structure requires skilled stonemasons, who are being assisted by youngsters from Harlem.

In the gift shop there's a wonderful model of the cathedral as the architect must have imagined it.

Harlem (off map)

Reaching north to the Harlem River, south to 110th St., east to Fifth Ave and west to Morningside and St Nicholas Aves. Subway: A, C, 3, 4, 5 or 6 to 125th St

Predominantly white throughout the 19th century, Harlem didn't see blacks settling in until 1900. It is now one of the best-known black communities in America, if not in the world. During the first half of the 20th century, the residents of Harlem did more to establish and popularize black arts, music and literature than virtually any group before them, with such distinguished names as W.E.B. DuBois, Langston Hughes, Malcolm X, Louis Armstrong, Bessie Smith, Charlie Parker, Thelonius

Monk and Dizzy Gillespie either living here or performing in the clubs. The Depression, however, took a heavy toll on the neighbourhood, leaving it with a high crime rate, drug abuse, poverty and homelessness.

Today, fortunately, Harlem is back on its feet again: several museums have opened, 125th St—the major commercial area in the neighbourhood—is hosting more and more stores, the Apollo Theater (253 West 125th St) has been renovated, and many of the elegant brownstones have been refurbished.

Accompanied walking tours of the neighbourhood are available. Don't miss Striver's Row on West 138th and 139th Sts, between Seventh and Eighth Aves.

Studio Museum in Harlem (off map)

144 West 125th St
Subway: A, B, C or D to 125th St
Wed–Fri 10 a.m.–5 p.m.,
Sat–Sun 1 p.m.–6 p.m.
Tel. (212) 864-4500

Founded in 1968, the Studio Museum boasts an impressive collection of paintings, sculptures and photographs devoted entirely to African-American culture.

Two exhibits in particular stand out: a collection of photographs of

Harlem in the 1930s by James Van Der Zee, and the sculptures in the garden just outside the museum— this is another of the many magical little hideaways that New York's better museums have created for their visitors. Have a look at the stunning glass-bead jewellery in the funky gift shop.

Abyssinian Baptist Church (off map)

132 West 138th St
(between Adam Clayton Powell
and Malcolm X blvds
Subway: 1 or 9 to 137th St
Tel. (212) 872-7474

Known for its rousing gospel choir, this 1923 Gothic church was home for many years to the sermons of Adam Clayton Powell, the local preacher and congressman. It is worth attending Sunday services if you can.

George Washington Bridge (off map)

Architect Le Corbusier called it "the only seat of grace in this disorderly city". The bridge connects the Upper West Side of Manhattan to New Jersey. It spans 1067 m (3,500 ft) and its two decks support some 50 million cars a year. But on opening day in 1931 the first to cross over the bridge were two boys on roller skates!

Enough steel wire was used in its construction to stretch halfway to the moon.

Cloisters (off map)

Fort Tryon Park
Subway: A to 190th St./
Washington Ave
Bus: Shuttle from Metropolitan
Museum
March–Oct, Tues–Sun
9.30 a.m.–5.15 p.m.;
Nov–Feb, Tues–Sun 9.30 a.m.–
4.45 p.m.
Tel. (212) 923-3700

The location offers welcome respite from the busy city streets. For lovers of the medieval, the Cloisters is an enchanting place to spend a few hours. The museum is a branch of the Metropolitan Museum of Art, and comprises five French and Spanish medieval monasteries, a Romanesque chapel and a 12th-century Spanish apse. Among the extraordinary exhibits, you'll admire a series of late medieval tapestries depicting a unicorn hunt, a 12th-century Romanesque cross with more than 100 carved figures, endless panes of 15th- and 16th-century stained-glass and rare illuminated manuscripts dating back almost 800 years. The courtyard gardens and view of the Hudson River and New Jersey should not be missed.

OTHER BOROUGHS

With all of Manhattan vying for your attention, it's easy to forget about the city's four outlying boroughs: the Bronx, Queens, Brooklyn and Staten Island. But you'd be missing out if you stayed in Manhattan exclusively during your trip.

The Bronx

The Bronx's reputation as a high-crime area makes many tourists think twice. Certainly, it has its problems—poverty, homelessness, drug abuse—but it's definitely improving. Immigrants from Latin America, Korea, Vietnam and Pakistan are settling in the area, opening new businesses and renovating long-ignored apartment buildings. And though many continue to associate it with urban blight, the 109-sq-km (42-sq-mile) Bronx surprisingly boasts more parkland than any other borough, almost a quarter of the total land.

New York Botanical Gardens

2300 Southern Blvd
Metro North Harlem line
(from Grand Central Station) to
Botanical Gardens
Tues–Sun 10 a.m.–6 p.m.
(extended hours in summer)
Tel. (718) 817-8700

One of the few "true escapes" in the city, the gardens are home to the largest surviving stand of virgin forest that, centuries ago, used to cover all of New York City. The 100-ha (250-acre) park also boasts walking paths, an arboretum, a herbarium (with some 6 million specimens of dried plants), a spectacular rose garden, a world-class conservatory and a moderately priced restaurant with excellent food.

Bronx Zoo/International Wildlife Conservation Park

Fordham Rd/Bronx River Parkway
Subway: 2 to Pelham Parkway
Mon–Fri 10 a.m.–5 p.m.;
Sat–Sun to 5.30 p.m.
Tel. (718) 367-1010

Make your way through one of biggest zoos in the country on foot, tram, monorail or shuttlebus. You'll find no mountain tigers pacing back and forth inside steel cages in this zoo—its 4,000 animals socialize, sleep and eat in "natural habitats". Zoo highlights include the Jungleworld, the World of Darkness, and the Congo Gorilla Forest.

Queens

This is the largest borough in the city, the size of Manhattan, the Bronx and Staten Island combined.

And in terms of immigration, it's what Manhattan was at the end of the 19th century: a stunning 36 per cent of Queens residents are foreign-born. Asians, Greeks and Latin Americans, Haitians and Romanians have established distinct ethnic communities here. Queens is largely residential, and has been spared the traffic congestion, noise, and over-development of Manhattan and other boroughs. If you're in the area, you visit the Isamu Noguchi Garden Museum at 32 Vernon Boulevard; tel. (718) 204-7088, and the MoMA (see p. 34).

Brooklyn

With more residents (almost 2.5 million) than any other of New York's boroughs, an area of 210 sq km (80 sq miles), its own bustling business district, beautiful parks and world-famous museums, Brooklyn is a city unto itself. Until 1898, it was entirely independent of New York City. Today, the borough that sits just across the East River—particularly Brooklyn Heights and Park Slope—continues to attract Manhattan residents, partly because the rents are less expensive, the streets quieter and the atmosphere more communal. Brooklyn is also quite accessible to tourists, a 10-minute subway ride from Manhattan or a 20-minute stroll across Brooklyn Bridge.

Brooklyn Museum of Art

:: 200 Eastern Parkway
:: Subway: 2 or 3 to Eastern Parkway/Brooklyn Museum
:: Wed–Fri and Sun
:: 10 a.m.–5 p.m., Sat to 9 p.m.
:: Tel. (718) 638-5000

The second-largest museum in New York boasts a collection of almost 1.5 million pieces. The Egyptian, African and pre-Columbian art collections are world-renowned, and the period rooms are a looking-glass into another era. Find out what the living room of a 17th-century New York farmhouse looked like, or step inside the Moorish Room of John D. Rockefeller's midtown mansion, complete with exotic tiles, brocaded walls and wood paneling.
Works by Georgia O'Keeffe are displayed in the Gallery of American Painting and Sculpture. The sculpture garden outside is a magical little nook.

Brooklyn Botanic Garden

:: 1000 Washington Ave
:: Subway: Q to Prospect Park
:: Tues–Fri 8 a.m.–4.30 p.m., Sat, Sun, holidays 10 a.m.–4.30 p.m.
:: Tel. (718) 623-7200

One-fifth the size of the garden in the Bronx, Brooklyn's petite version is just as impressive. Highlights include a Japanese Garden, Cranford Rose Garden (with 1,200 varieties), Shakespeare Garden (flowers featured in the Bard's plays) and greenhouses.

Prospect Park

:: Park Slope, Brooklyn
:: Subway: Q to Prospect Park

The park was designed by Frederick Law Olmstead and Calvert Vaux, the same team that drew up the plans for Central Park. Much like its cousin in Manhattan, the 213-ha (526-acre) park was spared the incursion of any city streets and the result is a quiet, green oasis amidst urban Brooklyn. The park's biggest attractions include its picnic areas, running paths, baseball diamonds, zoo, skating rink and an old Quaker cemetery where actor Montgomery Clift is buried.

Wildlife Center

:: Prospect Park, Brooklyn
:: Subway: Q to Prospect Park

Just the right size if you're not quite ready to tackle the enormous Bronx Zoo Conservation Park. The park is geared toward children, but the sea-lion pool, the discovery trail and the 160 creatures will hold adults' attention, too.

Verrazano-Narrows Bridge

With a 1,298-m (4,260-ft) span linking Staten Island to Brooklyn, the Verrazano-Narrows is one of the longest suspension bridges in the world. It was completed in 1964. The houses of many of the Italian-Americans living in Brooklyn were destroyed in order to make room for the bridge; in an attempt at reconciliation the city decided to name the structure after the Italian explorer Giovanni da Verrazano.

Staten Island

The least populated borough and the most homogeneous, both economically and politically. Less than 400,000 predominantly white and middle-class New Yorkers make their home here. A free ferry carries commuters and tourists to and from the island, offering one of the best views of the Statue of Liberty and the New York skyline.

Historic Richmond Town

- 441 Clarke Ave
- Bus S74 from ferry
- to Richmond (40 min.)
- Hours vary during the year.
- Tel. (718) 351-1611

A historic village and museum complex devoted to life on Staten Island. It comprises 27 original buildings, the oldest being Voorlezer House, c. 1695.

Jacques Marchais Museum of Tibetan Art

- 338 Lighthouse Ave
- Bus S74 from ferry to Lighthouse Ave
- Wed–Sun 1–5 p.m.
- Tel. (718) 987-3500

Authentic replica of a Himalayan monastery with a collection of Tibetan artefacts.

Alice Austen House and Garden

- 2 Hylan Blvd
- Bus S51 from ferry to Hylan Blvd
- Thurs–Sun noon–5 p.m.
- Tel. (718) 816-4506

Austen was one of the first American women to take up photography. Her house is now a museum of Victorian lifestyle, with a gallery of her photos. The garden looks out on the Narrows.

National Lighthouse Museum

- 1 Lighthouse Plaza
- From the ferry ramp, turn left.
- Tel. (718) 556-1681
- www.lighthouse.org

Several landmark buildings connected by esplanades to the ferry terminal. The museum is opening in phases as the buildings undergo renovation; they include the Administration Building, the old lampshop and the vaults.

Dining Out

The first real restaurant in New York City did not appear until 1831, when two Swiss brothers set up an establishment where local businessmen could come for a hot meal—the legendary Delmonico's. Today there are 10,000 restaurants in New York City. Some of the more expensive establishments require reservations, so it's best to phone ahead and check. And remember this simple trick when you're figuring out the tip, which is never included in the bill: just double the tax.

We have included cafés and coffeehouses in this section, for those who just want a quick snack or respite from shopping or sightseeing. Each of the restaurants is coded to give an approximate idea of the price per person for a meal. The categories are:

$	below $16	$$$	$31–$50
$$	$17–$30	$$$$	$50 or more

DOWNTOWN

Hudson River Club
4 World Financial Center
250 Vesey St (West St.)
Subway: 4, 5, A or C to Fulton St
Tel. (212) 786-1500
Splendid regional American cuisine and a panoramic view of the river compete for your attention at this high-priced downtown restaurant. $$$$

Gigino at Wagner Park
20 Battery Place (West St)
Subway: 4 or 5 to Bowling Green
Tel. (212) 528-2228
Fabulous harbour view, lots of atmosphere at this Italian in Battery Park City. $$$

City Hall
131 Duane St (between Church and West Broadway)
Subway: 1, 2, 3, 9, A or C to Chambers St
Tel. (212) 227-7777
Spacious, elegant American brasserie, with great photos of old New York on the walls and good food. $$$

ETHNIC NEW YORK

Baluchi's
193 Spring St., between Sullivan and Thompson
Subway: C or E to Spring St
Tel. (212) 226-2828
Exquisite Indian fare, and handy for a stroll through SoHo. If you have

come with a crowd, call ahead and ask for the private table downstairs. $$

Bar 89

89 Mercer St., between Broome and Spring Sts
Subway: 6 to Spring St
Tel. (212) 274-0989

If there exists such a thing as a chic salad, you'll find it here. Don't leave without winding your way past the willowy models munching on errant arugula leaves, up the stairs and into what are said to be the most spectacular WCs on the East Coast. $$

Bolo

23 East 22nd St
Subway: N or R to 23rd St
Tel. (212) 228-2200

More Art Deco than Madrid inside, and rather pricey. Nevertheless, it's a top contender for the city's best Spanish food—hearty, colourful and inspired. $$$

Café Mona Lisa

282 Bleecker St., between Jones St and Seventh Ave South
Subway: A, C, E, B, F or Q to West 4th St./Washington Square
Tel. (212) 929-1262

Tops for a café au lait or a quick snack. Don't miss out on the cheesecake.

Caffè Roma Pastry

385 Broome St at Mulberry
Subway: 6 to Spring St
Tel. (212) 226-8413

The Italian-style pastries are simply out of this world. Strictly forbidden if you're on a diet.

Caffè Reggio

119 MacDougal St., between Bleecker and West 3rd Sts
Subway: A, C, E, B, D, F or Q to West 4th St/Washington Square
Tel. (212) 475-9557

This is the oldest coffeehouse in Greenwich Village. Great espresso, great people-watching.

Country Café

69 Thompson St., between Broome and Spring Sts
Subway: C or E to Spring St
Tel. (212) 966-5417

It's either Moroccan cuisine with a heavy French influence, or the other way around. In any case, it's a gem of a restaurant. $$

Cupping Room Café

359 West Broadway between Broome and Grand Sts
Subway: A, C, E, 1 or 9 to Canal St
Tel. (212) 925-2898

The perfect spot for brunches. An omelette, a cup of coffee, and off you go, ready to tour SoHo.

Cyber Café

- 273 Lafayette St at Prince St
- Subway: N or R to Prince St or 6 to Spring St
- Tel. (212) 334-5140

As the name implies, it's part coffee bar, part information superhighway pit stop. Sip a mocha cappuccino and send an e-mail to your friends back home.

El Faro

- 823 Greenwich St at Horatio
- Subway: A, C or E to 14th St
- Tel. (212) 929-8210

The Elysian Fields of Spanish cuisine. Start with the sangria, following up with the paella, ribs or shrimp ajillo. Even the house salad is mouthwatering. $$

Gandhi

- 345 East 6th St
- Subway: N or R to Astor Place or 8th St
- Tel. (212) 614-9718

Of the plethora of Indian restaurants clamouring for your attention in these parts, Gandhi is the best. Excellent prices, too. $

Golden Unicorn

- 18 East Broadway at Catherine St
- Subway: N or R to Canal St
- Tel. (212) 941-0911

Great spot for a dim-sum Sunday brunch, but be sure to get there early. Take the lift to the third floor and, behold, Chinese dumpling heaven. $$

Gotham Bar & Grill

- 12 East 12th St
- Subway: N, R, 4, 5 or 6 to 14th St/Union Square
- Tel. (212) 620-4020

Best at midday, when prices are lowest for this fine New American cuisine (bargain $20 fixed price lunch). Growing more popular by the day. $$$

Hangawi

- 12 East 32nd St
- Subway: 6 to 33rd St
- Tel. (212) 213-0077

One of the premier Korean vegetarian restaurants in the city. Pillows double as seats and you have to remove your shoes, but no one seems to mind. $$$

Jekyll and Hyde Pub

- 91 Seventh Ave South, between Barrow and Grove Sts
- Subway: 1 or 9 to Christopher St, A, B, C, D, E, F or Q to West 4th St
- Tel. (212) 989-7285

A restaurant and club for explorers and mad scientists, or so they say. $

Joe's Shanghai

- 9 Pell St between Bowery and Mott Sts

You can eat all round the clock, and all round the world, in New York City.

Subway: 6 to Canal St
Tel. (212) 233-8888
They make the best dumplings in town. Expect crowds, but they somehow manage to squeeze everybody inside. $$

Kang Suh Restaurant

1250 Broadway at 32nd St
Subway: N, R, B, D, F or Q to 34th St
Tel. (212) 564-6845
Platters of tender marinated raw meats and seafood and a grill in the centre of the table make for a sumptuous cook-it-yourself meal. $$

Kin Khao

171 Spring St (between Thompson and West Broadway)
Subway: C or E to Spring St
Tel. (212) 966-3939
The queue can be a bit long for dinner, but it's well worth the wait. Excellent Thai curries and other spicy dishes made with coconut milk are prepared in full view of the diners. Loud and boisterous atmosphere. $$

Knickerbocker Bar & Grill

33 University Place and 9th St
Subway: N or R to Astor Place
Tel. (212) 228-8490

Superb steak and potatoes spot in Greenwich Village. Prices are low, and they often host jazz bands at dinnertime. $$

Le Figaro Café
184 Bleecker St at MacDougal
Subway: A, C, E, B, D, F or Q to West 4th St/Washington Square
Tel. (212) 677-1100
The staff is a bit slow, but there are plenty of interesting characters to distract you while you wait. Great pastries.

Le Gamin
183 9th Ave at 21st St
Subway: C or R to 23rd St
Tel. (212) 243-8854
Another branch at 50 MacDougal St., between Houston and Prince Sts
Small, cosy French cafés, reputed for their crepes and quiches.

Lombardi's
32 Spring St
between Mott and Mulberry Sts
Subway: 6 to Spring St
Tel. (212) 941-7994
Famous Italian joint in SoHo. Its century-old reputation is bolstered by the inimitable clam pizza. $

Moustache
90 Bedford St, between Barrow and Grove Sts

Subway: 1 or 9 to Sheridan Square
Tel. (212) 229-2220
Middle Eastern restaurant, prized for their fragrant, crispy "pitzas" and low prices. $

The Odeon
145 West Broadway
Subway: 1, 2, 3 or 9 to Chambers St
Tel. (212) 233-0507
Legendary TriBeCa hot spot that is still "in". Good American-French fare. Best late night, when the arty folk show up. $$$

Nha Trang
87 Baxter St, between Bayard and Canal Sts
Subway: N, R or 6 to Spring St
Tel. (212) 233-5948
Crowded, rushed, a bit drab and dingy but, without a doubt, the best place in Manhattan for Vietnamese food. The spring rolls are a must. $

Union Square Café
21 East 16th St
Subway: N, R, 4, 5 or 6 to 14th St/Union Square
Tel. (212) 243-4020
Local food critics can't praise this place enough. The New American cuisine is exemplary, the atmosphere classy, the service perfect. $$$

Village Ma

107 MacDougal St, between Bleecker and West 3rd St
Subway: A, B, C, D, E, F or Q to West 4th St/ Washington Square
Tel. (212) 529-3808

Thai cuisine in a jungle-like setting.

MIDTOWN

Aquavit

13 West 54th St
Subway: E or F to 53rd St
Tel. (212) 307-7311

Excellent Scandinavian restaurant boasting an extensive list of aquavits, smoked meats and seafood. $$$$

Barbetta

321 West 46th St
Subway: A, C or E to 42nd St
Tel. (212) 246-9171

Serving up some of the best Italian food in the city for almost a century, this is the perfect spot for dinner if you're heading off to a Broadway show afterwards. $$$

Cabana Carioca

123 West 45th St
Subway: N, R, 1, 2, 3 or 9 to 42nd St
Tel. (212) 581-8088
toll-free 800-246-8091

Garlic-laden, hearty Brazilian fare with the emphasis on seafood and

PIZZERIAS

In recent years, some up-scale pizzerias have been trying to capture a slice of New York's pizza market. They usually offer a fancy, wafer-thin crust or pile six or seven pounds of vegetables on top of a normal cheese pie and call it "Garden Pizza". Don't be fooled. The proper—and by far the best—pizza can still be found in the cheap, seedy pizza joints lining the avenues. Some of the best:

- **Five Roses Pizza**: 173 First Ave (between 10th and 11th Sts),
  subway: L to First Ave.
- **Joe's Pizza**: 233 Bleecker St at Carmine St, subway: A, C or E to W. 9th St
- **John's Pizzeria**: 408 East 64th St, subway: 6 to 68th St.
- **Original Ray's Pizza**: 2607 Broadway at 98th St,
  subway: 1, 2 or 3 to 96th St.
- **Patsy's Pizza**: 61 W. 74th St (between Columbus Ave and
  Central Park W.), subway: 1, 2 or 3 to 72nd St.
- **Stromboli's**: 112 University Place (between 11th and 12th Sts),
  subway: N or R to 14th St.
- **Vinnie's Pizza**: 285 Amsterdam Ave(between 73rd and 74th Sts),
  subway: 1, 2 or 3 to 72nd St.

steaks; perfect for a pre-theatre dinner if you're looking for exotic flavours at a reasonable price. $$

Café Centro

- 200 Park Ave, between 45th St and Vanderbilt Ave
- Subway: 4, 5, 6 to 42nd St
- S from Times Square
- Tel. (212) 818-1222

Lively French-Mediterranean brasserie next to Grand Central Station.

Four Seasons

- 99 East 52nd St
- Subway: 6 to 51st, E or F to 53rd St
- Tel. (212) 754-9494

A New York institution, catering to the rich and famous. The menu touches on classic American and international cuisine. Jackets (and life-savings) required, reservations essential. $$$$

Hard Rock Café

- 221 West 57th St
- Subway: N or R to 57th St
- Tel. (212) 489-6565

The queues are long, the place is teeming with tourists, the food ("casual American fare") is mediocre, but most people seem to put up with all that just to be able to say they went to the Hard Rock Café. $$

Lutèce

- 249 East 50th St
- Subway: 6 to 51st St
- Tel. (212) 752-2225

The quintessential New York French bistro, with new, updated contemporary food, a spruced-up decor and fixed price $38 lunch; fabulous value. Make reservations well in advance. $$$$

Manhattan Ocean Club

- 57 West 58th St
- Subway: B or Q to 57th St
- Tel. (212) 371-7777

This is considered one of the best seafood restaurants in the city, and all its products are extraordinarily fresh. $$$$

Rainbow Room

- General Electric Building, 30 Rockefeller Plaza, between 49th and 50th Sts
- Subway: B, D, F or Q to Rockefeller Center/49th St
- Tel. (212) 632-5100

An elegant venue for an extra-special night out. The oysters and lobster are exquisite, and when you can take your eyes off the plate, the view of Manhattan from the 65th floor is inspiring. $$$$

Rock Center Café

- Rockefeller Center, Skating Rink
- 20 West 50th St

Subway: B, D, F or Q to
47th/50th St/Rockefeller Center
Tel. (212) 332-7620
In the Christmas season, you'll have
a cheery view of the skaters in
Rockefeller Center and the
Christmas tree. The food, however,
plays second fiddle to the view. $$$

Russian Samovar
256 West 52nd St (between
Broadway and Eighth Ave)
Subway: B, D or E to 53rd St
or 1, 9 to 49th St
Tel. (212) 757-0168
Gastronomic glasnost in the heart
of the theatre district. A fine choice
for a plate of beef stroganoff. Sing-
along pianist after 9 p.m. $$

Smith & Wollensky
797 Third Ave at 49th St
Subway: 6 to 51st St
Tel. (212) 753-1530
A New York institution famous for
its porterhouse steak dinners, fine
wines and after-dinner cigars. $$$

Zarela
953 Second Ave,
between 50th and 51st Sts
Subway: 6 to 51st St
Tel. (212) 644-6740
Top-rated Mexican eats and the
best margaritas in town; perfect for
lunch if you've just toured the UN.
$$

UPTOWN

Avenue Bistro
520 Columbus Ave,
corner of 85th St
Subway: 1, 9 to 86th St
Tel. (212) 579-3194
Ideal for brunch; sophisticated
French-American fare in the
evening. Excellent desserts. $$

Café Con Leche
424 Amsterdam Ave,
between 80th and 81st Sts
Subway: 1, 9 to 79th St
Tel. (212) 595-7000
Sumptuous Cuban food that will
make you wish you could hop
straight onto a plane for Havana.
$$

Café des Artistes
1 West 67th St., between
Columbus Ave and Central Park
West
Subway: 1 or 9 to 66th St
Tel. (212) 877-3500
French cuisine of the highest order
and one of the most romantic
interiors in the city have placed
Café des Artistes at the summit. The
steak tartare and raw oysters are
delectable. $$$$

Carlyle Restaurant
Carlyle Hotel
35 East 76th St

Subway: 6 to 77th St
Tel. (212) 744-1600
Fancy décor, with Fortuny fabric-covered walls and engravings by Redoute, classic French cuisine, impeccable service and sky-high prices in one of the city's most expensive hotels. $$$$

JEWISH DELIS AND BAGEL STORES

For New York Jews, there are three interests in life: synagogue, Palestinian-Israeli relations, and bagels with lox. The delis and bagel stores listed below are widely considered the best for takeaway bagels and sit-down meals.

– **Carnegie Deli**: 854 Seventh Ave at 55th St, subway: N, R to 57th St.
– **Ess-a-Bagel**: 359 First Ave at 21st St., subway: 6 to 23rd St.
– **H&H Bagels West**: 1551 Second Ave, between 80th and 81st Sts, subway: 4,6 to 86th St.
– **Katz's Deli**: 205 East Houston St at Ludlow St, subway: F to Second Ave.
– **Ratner's Deli**: 138 Delancey St between Norfolk and Suffolk Sts, subway: F to Delancey St.
– **Second Avenue Deli**: 156 Second Ave at 10th St, subway: L to First Ave or 6 to Astor Place

Jo-An Japanese

2707 Broadway
between 103rd and 104th Sts
Subway: 1 or 9 to 103rd St
Tel. (212) 678-2103
Excellent and inexpensive sushi. An ideal spot to stop if you're in the Upper West Side. Booking advised on weekdays. $$

Le Bilboquet

25 East 63rd St
Subway: B or Q to 63rd St,
N or R to Fifth Ave
Tel. (212) 751-3036
Small French restaurant on the Upper East Side which, on a busy night, turns into a crush.
The dishes are superb, the wine list excellent. $$$

Pamir

1437 Second Ave,
between 74th and 75th Sts
Subway: 6 to 77th St
Tel. (212) 734-3791
Another branch at 1065 First Ave at 58th St
The tasty giant shish kebabs at these Afghan restaurants should be patented. $$

Pesce Pasta Tre

1562 Third Ave,
between 87th and 88th Sts
Subway: 4, 5 or 6 to 86th St
Tel. (212) 987-4696

As the name implies, excellent pasta and above-average fish dishes are among the highlights at this Italian spot. $$

Sylvia's

328 Lenox Ave,
between 126th and 127th Sts
Subway: 2 or 3 to 125th St
Tel. (212) 996-0660

By far the best soul food (ribs, fried chicken, fresh vegetables) in the northeast US. It's inexpensive, too. $$

Tavern on the Green

Central Park West and 66th St
Subway: B or C to 72nd St

New York extravagance; fabulous terrace in summer. The American cooking definitely takes a back seat to the decor, but the tavern is an "experience". $$$

Zen Palate

2170 Broadway,
between 76th and 77th Sts
Subway: 1 or 9 to 79th St
Tel. (212) 501-7768
Other branches: 663 9th Ave at 46th St and
34 Union Square East

This trio of Asian-style restaurants cooks up light and extraordinarily flavourful dishes. An essential stop for vegetarians or anyone looking for something light. $$

BROOKLYN

Al Di La

248 Fifth Ave (Carroll St.)
Subway: R to Union St
Tel. (718) 783-4565

Delicious Venetian cooking at Brooklyn prices. No reservations, so go early or be prepared to wait. $$$

A Table

171 Lafayette Ave (Adelphi St)
Subway: R to Union St
Tel. (718) 935-9121

Small French bistro with Parisian vibes and communal tables. $$$

Peter Luger Steak House

178 Broadway (Driggs Ave)
Brooklyn
Taxi recommended
Tel. (718) 387-7400

If you're fond of meat, call at Peter Luger's, one of the oldest and best steak houses in the country. You'll be served a piece of meat the size of half a cow. $$$

River Café

1 Water St
Subway: A or C to High St,
or take a cab
Tel. (718) 522-5200

Priceless view of Manhattan, American menu. Fixed price only (dinner $70), but open daily for lunch as well as Sunday brunch.

Entertainment

Once the sun sets, New York becomes another creature altogether and your options multiply. You can see some world-class opera at Lincoln Center, catch a film at the venerable Ziegfeld Theater or hit a Broadway show. Have a drink at a smoky downtown tavern or check out an up-and-coming punk band in the East Village. A good tip: keep an extra $15 on hand to take a taxi if you're out late. The *New Yorker, Time Out, The New York Times* and the "Voice Choice" section of *The Village Voice* all have detailed "what's on" information.

BALLET, OPERA, CLASSICAL MUSIC

Most of the city's classical performances take place at Lincoln Center, a complex of several buildings at Broadway and 65th St. The New York State Theater (home to the NYC Ballet and the NYC Opera) is the southernmost building; the Metropolitan Opera House is in the centre, and Avery Fisher Hall to the north.

For tickets, telephone Centercharge at (212) 721-6500 or TicketMaster at (212) 307-4100 or go directly to the box office.

American Ballet Theatre

- Lincoln Center
- Metropolitan Opera House
- Subway: 1 or 9 to 66th St
- Tel. (212) 362-6000

Since 1940, this dance company has enthralled audiences with classics like *The Sleeping Beauty, La Bayardere* and *Swan Lake.* Rudolf Nureyev, Mikhail Baryshnikov and Cynthia Gregory have all graced the stage.

Carnegie Hall

- 57th St and Seventh Ave
- Subway: N or R to 57th St
- Tel. (212) 247-7800

Perhaps the most splendid concert hall in the country. The Carnegie is best known for hosting world-famous orchestras, but jazz, folk-music and rock bands (notably the Beatles) have played here.

Metropolitan Opera House

- Lincoln Center
- Subway: 1 or 9 to 66th St
- Tel. (212) 362-6000

The Met attracts the brightest stars of the operatic heavens: Pavarotti, Cecilia Bartoli, Placido Domingo and Kathleen Battle, among others.

New York City Ballet
- Lincoln Center
- New York State Theater
- Subway: 1 or 9 to 66th St
- Tel. (212) 870-5570

Another venerated city ballet company. George Balanchine's *The Nutcracker* is staged during the Christmas season.

New York City Opera
- Lincoln Center
- New York State Theater
- Subway: 1 or 9 to 66th St
- Tel. (212) 870-5570

Like the Met, it stages the classic operas, though has begun to tackle more eclectic pieces as well.

New York Philharmonic
- Lincoln Center
- Avery Fisher Hall
- Subway: 1 or 9 to 66th St
- Tel. (212) 875-5656

Directed by conductor Kurt Masur since 1991, the New York Philharmonic satisfies the city's love for classical music, performing some 200 concerts per year.

BARS

ArtBar
- 52 Eighth Ave,
- between Horatio and Jane Sts
- Subway: A, E, C to 14th St
- Tel. (212) 727-0244

The best time to call at the ArtBar is late afternoon. Go all the way to the back. Excellent White Russians.

Barrymore's
- 267 West 45th St
- Subway: any 42nd St stop
- Tel. (212) 391-8400

Hobnob with theatre folk and admire the poster collection.

Café Un Deux Trois
- 123 West 44th St
- Subway: any 42nd St stop
- Tel. (212) 354-4148

A former hotel lobby catering to chic midtown residents and post-theatre crowds. There are crayons on every table so you can idle away the time by colouring in the tablecloths.

Corner Bistro
- 331 West 4th St at Jane St
- Subway: A, C, E to 14th St
- Tel. (212) 242-9502

Fabulous hamburgers and chips, locally brewed McSorley's Ale, a variety of choice scotches and one of the best jukeboxes in the city have made this an institution.

Dakota Bar and Grill
- 1576 Third Ave,
- between 88th and 89th Sts
- Subway: 4, 5, 6 to 86th St
- Tel. (212) 427-8889

Young professionals and a post-college crowd line up along the Dakota's 52-ft bar.

Landmark Tavern

626 11th Ave at 46th St
Subway: A, C, E to 42nd St
Tel. (212) 757-8595

Frequented by an older, more sophisticated crowd. Each of the three floors is fitted with a fireplace.

McSorley's Old Ale House

15 East 7th St
Subway: 6 to Astor Place
Tel. (212) 473-9148

Here they have been serving up mugs of home-brewed ale since 1854 in a fantastic old-tavern atmosphere.

Mona's

224 Ave B,
between 13th and 14th Sts
Subway: N, R, 4, 5 or 6 to 14th St
Tel. (212) 353-3780

As grungy as they get, but offering a glimpse of self-destructive East Village culture. There's no sign outside, but it's the only bar on the block.

White Horse Tavern

567 Hudson St at 11th St
Subway: A, C or E to 14th St
Tel. (212) 989-3956

Fabled West Village watering hole, where Dylan Thomas and friends drank themselves to death. Dark and crowded, serving an increasingly young, professional crowd.

CONTEMPORARY MUSIC

Brownies

169 Avenue A
Subway: L to First Ave,
6 to Astor Place
Tel. (212) 420-8392

East Village classic, cool live music and weekly DJ nights. Basic decor.

CBGB

315 Bowery St at Bleecker St
Subway: B, D, F, Q to
Broadway/Lafayette St.;
6 to Bleecker St
Tel. (212) 982-4052

Since 1975, CBGB has been at the top of the charts. The full name is CBGB (& OMFUG) which stands for Country, Bluegrass, Blues and Other Music for Uplifting Gourmandizers.

Knitting Factory

74 Leonard St., between
Church St and Broadway
Subway: A, C E, N, R, 6 to Canal
St.; 1, 9 to Franklin St
Tel. (212) 219-3055

A great spot for alternative music, the real thing.

Mercury Lounge

217 Houston St at Essex St
Subway: F or V to Lower East
Side/Second Ave
Tel. (212) 260-4700

One of the best sound systems in
NYC. A real music lover's venue
showcasing up and coming rock
bands.

Paddy Reilly's Music Bar

519 Second Ave at 29th St
Subway: 6 to 28th St
Tel. (212) 686-1210

A warm, friendly crowd gathers on
Thursday nights for traditional Irish
folk music.

JAZZ AND BLUES CLUBS

Arthur's Tavern

57 Grove St at Seventh Ave South
Subway: 1, 9 to Christopher St/
Sheridan Square
Tel. (212) 675-6879

Dixieland jazz on Sunday and
Monday, a slower moodier swing
the rest of the week.

Birdland

315 West 44th St
Subway: A, C, E to 42nd St
Tel. (212) 581-3080

Named after Charlie "Bird" Parker,
this venue has hosted the likes of
Dizzy Gillespie, Count Basie and
Bud Powell. Still attracts the best.

THEATRE

The more established playwrights
generally grab the stages on
Broadway and the Times Square
area, while the up-and-coming
are relegated to Off-Broadway
and elsewhere in town. Discount
tickets (sometimes up to 50% off)
for most shows are available at
the Theater Development Fund,
located at Times Square and 47th
St. In order to qualify for the discount, you need to buy the tickets
on the day of the performance.

Blue Note

131 West 3rd St
Subway: N, R to 8th St;
6 to Bleecker St
Tel. (212) 475-8592

The most venerated jazz club in the
city. Heavy cover charge, but expect
to be blown away.

Terra Blues

149 Bleecker St, between
Thompson and LaGuardia
Subway: any to 4th St/
Washington Square,
6 to Bleecker St
Tel. (212) 777-7776

Comfortable and friendly, down
home blues.

The Bottom Line

15 West 4th St
Subway: N or R to 8th St;

6 to Bleecker St
Tel. (212) 228-6300
This perennial blues spot in the West Village has made a habit of catching rising stars.

Village Vanguard

178 Seventh Ave South at 11th St
Subway: 1, 2, 3 or 9 to 14th St
Tel. (212) 255-4037
Pulled in John Coltrane, Thelonius Monk and Charles Mingus in its heyday and it's still cookin'.

DANCELAND

Baktun

418 West 14th St
Subway: A, C or E to 14th St;
L to Eighth Ave
Tel. (212) 206-1590
Young crowd. Everything from house to bizarre Indian tunes.

Centro-Fly

45 West 21st St
Subway: F, N, R or V to 23rd St
Tel. (212) 627-7770
House music, glossy Flatiron nightspot. An intimate, loungey club with psychedelic decor and gogo girls. Food served till 5 a.m.

Filter 14

432 West 14th St
Subway: A, C, E, 1, 2, 3, 9 to 14th St
Tel. (212) 366-5680

Hardly glitzy; house music and DJs in three run-down rooms.

Lucky Cheng's

24 First Ave,
between 1st and 2nd Sts
Subway: F to Second Ave
Tel. (212) 473-0516
All ethnicities and orientations come here to flaunt their stuff to 80s disco and 90s hip-hop.

Sound Factory

618 West 46th St
Subway: A, C E to 50th St
Tel. (212) 489-0001
Two floors, one given over to House, the other to 80s retro-pop. $20 to get in and sweat.

Vinyl

6 Hubert St at Hudson St
Subway: A, C or E to Canal St,
1 or 2 to Franklin St
Tel. (212) 625-1717
Big-name DJs, super sound system. Sunday afternoon body and soul party.

Webster Hall

125 East 11th St
Subway: N, R, 4, 5 or 6 to
14th St/Union Square
Tel. (212) 353-1600
Fve separate floors, each with a distinctive style of music. Trapeze artists and occasional live music.

The Hard Facts

Accommodation

It's best to make your hotel reservations well in advance of your arrival. If, for some reason, you find yourself in Manhattan with nowhere to stay, call in at the NYC&Co at 810 Seventh Ave at 53rd St. Tel. (212) 484-1222. Open weekdays 9 a.m.–6 p.m., and Saturday and Sunday 10 a.m.–6 p.m. It publishes a list of hotels in the city, with approximate rates, locations and phone numbers. Keep in mind that the listed rates for hotel rooms do not include a 19% tax and a $2 per day occupancy tax.

Airports

Three airports serve the New York City area:

**John F. Kennedy (JFK)
International Airport**
(Queens)
Tel. (718) 244-4444

Newark International Airport
(New Jersey)
Tel. (973) 961-6000

LaGuardia Airport
(Queens)
Tel. (718) 533-3400

One of the most disconcerting aspects of your trip to New York might well be figuring out how to get from the airport to your hotel. After you've claimed your luggage and made it through customs, you'll see signs everywhere announcing the various modes of transportation to New York City. JFK and Newark International airports are huge complexes, and even New Yorkers lose their way if they're not careful.

One of the simplest ways to and from the local airports is by yellow cab. Rates for the ride from JFK have been standardized: $35 to any destination in Manhattan, not including tolls (about $4) and tip. Taxis from Newark International Airport usually cost $25–$30, not including tolls and tip. A cab from LaGuardia Airport will run $20–$26, depending on traffic conditions, not including tolls and tip.

The next best bet is by bus. Relatively cheap (about $13–$15 from any of the airports), they will take you to midtown Manhattan, where you can get a taxi to your hotel. The following companies service all of the airports:

Gray Line Air Shuttle
Tel. (212) 315-3006

New York Airport Service
Tel. (212) 875-8200

Olympia Airport Express
Tel. (212) 964-6233

To return to the airport, the same bus companies take passengers from midtown (southeast corner of Park Ave and 42nd St.) to the three major airports. Of course, you can always catch a taxi, though the same standardized fare doesn't apply for the return trip to JFK. Expect to pay about $40 to JFK and Newark International and $25 to LaGuardia Airport, inclusive of tip and tolls.

The new AirTrain rail system enables you to avoid road traffic. At present only AirTrain Newark is functioning; it connects with NJ TRANSIT and Amtrak trains at the Newark International Airport station. The two AirTrain JFK services will open in late 2002 and early 2003. For more specific information see:
www.njtransit.com

Business Hours
The city never sleeps—you can get a meal, buy toothpaste, cigarettes, medication or a bouquet of flowers at 3 a.m. if you like. Shops generally open from 10 a.m. to 6 p.m., Monday to Saturday. Some open Sunday for a few hours, though it's best to call ahead and check. The large department stores often remain open well into the evening (9 or 10 p.m.) and many open on Sunday as well.

Banks open Mon–Fri 9 a.m.–3 or 3.30 p.m. A few branches may stay open late on Thursday or Friday and some open for a few hours on Saturday morning.

Climate
The best seasons for visiting New York are spring and autumn. In summer, June, July and August, temperatures average 25–28°C (77–82°F) but may reach extremes of 39°C (102°F)! The coldest winter months are January and February, with temperatures averaging around 0°C (32°F). (Americans still measure temperatures in Fahrenheit.)

Consulates
British citizens requiring consular assistance can get in touch with their Consul:
845 Third Avenue, NY 10022
tel. (212) 745-0200
fax (212) 745-3062
The British Embassy, in Washington, D.C., handles more serious matters:
tel. (212) 745 0202
see also:
www.britainusa.com

The Australian Consulate General is at
150 East 42nd St
34th floor
NY 1017
tel. (212) 315-6500
fax (212) 351-6501
www.australiaNYC.org
Canadian Consulate:
1251 Ave of the Americas
NY 10020
tel. (212) 596-1628
fax (212) 596-1793

Canadian citizens needing consular help can call collect:
(613) 996 8885
or e-mail sos@dfait-maeci.gc.ca

Customs and Entry Formalities

It's essential that you check with your local US consulate or embassy before your trip, to see what is required for entry into the US. Nationals of the USA and Canada, and holders of British passports endorsed "British citizen" do not need a visa.

No meat or plant products may be imported, and carrying drugs will get you into a lot of trouble. Security controls have been strongly reinforced since the September 2001 terrorist attacks.

Disabled

The Big Apple Visitors Guide, available from NYC&Co. (see Accommodation), is coded to show which landmarks, museums, restaurants, hotels, etc. are wheelchair accessible or have services for the visually impaired or hard-of-hearing. For subway users who are unable to enter through the turnstiles, the token-booth clerk will open a special gate. Buses are equipped with a wheelchair lift near the middle of the vehicle.

Driving

Driving in the traffic-clogged streets of New York is to be avoided at all costs, but if you're interested in exploring upstate New York, a car is indeed useful. The toll-free numbers of the major rental agencies are listed below. When you ask for prices, make sure they quote you the all-inclusive fee, complete with taxes and insurance charges.

Avis: Tel. (800) 331-1212

Budget: Tel. (800) 527-0700

Hertz: Tel. (800) 654-3131

Electric Current

The standard electrical current in the US is 110 volt 60-cycle AC. Travellers with alarm clocks, hair-dryers, rechargeable batteries or electric razors should invest in a transformer and an adapter plug before leaving home. Otherwise, any Radio Shack (a chain of electric appliance stores, listed in the phone book) is bound to have what you need.

Emergencies

To call an ambulance, a police officer or a fireman, dial 911 from the nearest phone. No coins are necessary and the service is available 24 hours a day.

Here are three of New York's major hospitals:

St Vincent's Hospital
11th St and Seventh Ave
Tel. (212) 604-8000

St Luke's Roosevelt
1000 Tenth Ave
Tel. (212) 523-6800

NYU Medical Center
540 First Ave
Tel. (212) 263-7300

Note that if you are admitted to hospital you may be required to pay a deposit in cash.

If you lose a filling, you can telephone Metropolitan Dental Association, (212) 732-7400, open 7 days a week, or AAAA Dental Care, tel. (212) 744 3928, open 24 hours a day, 7 days a week.

Lost Property

If you lose anything on a bus or in the subway, telephone the New York City Transit Authority at (212) 690-9638. If you leave something in a taxi, call NYC Taxi & Limousine Commission Lost Property at (212) 692-8294.

Media

To learn what's going on in the US and throughout the world, the best paper in town is The New York Times. For information on show times, concerts, gallery and museum exhibitions and music festivals, your best bets are *Time Out*, the *Village Voice*, *The New Yorker* or the Arts & Leisure section of the Sunday issue of *The New York Times*. News is broadcast, almost to excess, on most television channels. Try CNN if you're watching cable TV. Almost all newsstands and magazine stores stock newspapers and magazines from round the world.

Money Matters

The US dollar ($) is divided into 100 cents (¢). Coins are 1¢ (penny), 5¢ (nickel), 10¢ (dime) and 25¢ (quarter), with 50¢ (half-dollar) and $1 coins encountered infrequently. Banknotes in general circulation are $1, $5, $10, $20, $50 and $100. You would do well to depend on travellers cheques and a credit card, with a little cash for small expenditures. When you cash travellers cheques, $20 bills are the handiest: a rash of counterfeiting has made many merchants wary of $50 and $100 notes. It's a good idea to keep some change in your pockets, in case you want to hop on a bus or make a phone call.

The larger banks in the midtown area will exchange foreign currency, as will the exchange counters at the three major airports. Chase Manhattan Bank has hundreds of branches scattered throughout New York, all of which will exchange foreign currency. Two of the more accessible branches are located at Madison Ave and 42nd St and Fifth Ave and 43rd St., both near Grand Central Station.

Automated Teller Machines (ATMs) can be found everywhere in Manhattan, and many of them operate 24 hours a day.

Pharmacies
If you need medicines or toiletries, try one of the pharmacies listed below:

Boyds of Madison Ave
655 Madison Ave at 60th St
Tel. (212) 838-6558
Mon–Fri 8.30 a.m.–7.30 p.m., Sat 9.30 a.m.–7 p.m., Sun noon–6 p.m.

Duane Reade
405 Lexington at 42nd St
Tel. (212) 808-4743
Open 24 hours a day

Genovese
Second Ave and 68th St
Tel. (212) 772-0104
Open 24 hours a day.

Post Offices
Post offices are generally open Mon–Fri 10 a.m. to 5 or 6 p.m. The biggest—and the busiest—post office is located at 421 Eighth Ave, between 31st and 33rd Sts. It's open Mon–Fri, 24 hours a day.

Public Holidays
Instead of closing down, many stores take advantage of a federal (nationwide) holiday by having a sale. However, most museums, post offices and banks will shut their doors on the following holidays:

Jan. 1	New Year's Day
3rd Mon Jan.	Martin Luther King Day
3rd Mon Feb.	President's Day
Last Mon May	Memorial Day
July 4	Independence Day
1st Mon Sept.	Labor Day
2nd Mon Oct.	Columbus Day
Nov. 11	Veterans' Day
4th Tues Nov.	Thanksgiving Day
Dec. 25	Christmas Day

Public Transport

New York has one of the best public transport systems in the world. Laminated bus/subway maps are sold in most magazine stores, and free subway maps are available at stations.

For $1.50, you can travel to just about any point in the five boroughs. A MetroCard (sold at subway station booths, some banks and the occasional corner newsstand) allows access to and free transfers from buses and subways: $30 will give you 22 rides, which would last most people a week. Seven and 30-day unlimited ride MetroCards are also available.

Buses. The Manhattan buses run up or down the avenues (with the exception of Park Ave) and cross-town along the major two-way streets. Bus stops are indicated by small red-white-and-blue signs. In many cases, there are bus shelters near the signs. Either check your map or have a look at the rectangular box on the signpost to find out which route the bus follows.

When you board the bus, drop either $1.50 in coins or a token into the steel receptacle near the driver. If you have a MetroCard, insert it into the slot with the MetroCard icon. If you want to travel across town and then up- or down-town (or vice-versa), ask for a transfer when you board. To alight, press anywhere on one of the thin rubber strands running the length of the interior as you near your stop and the bus will pull over.

Subway. The subway operates 24 hours a day, and with your map in hand you can get to just about any point in the five boroughs on one fare. Buy a $1.50 token at the subway booth or use your MetroCard. Drop your token in the slot near the turnstile or swipe your MetroCard and walk through. When you use the subway, make sure to distinguish between an express train and a local; if you're not certain that the express stops where you want it to, take the local. Always stand well clear of the end of the platform, try to stick with the crowds after dark, avoid empty subway cars and don't use the subway at all late at night.

Taxis. Drivers of yellow taxi cabs are required by law to take you to any destination in the five boroughs. If the small box on the roof of the taxi is illuminated, the driver is free. He will pull over if you wave him down.

The cost for a taxi ride is $2 for the first 1/5 mile, 30 cents for each additional 1/5 mile, and 20 cents per minute if you're stuck in traffic. All rides between 8 p.m. and 6 a.m. carry an additional 50-cent surcharge, and all tolls are the passenger's responsibility. You can descend either on the right or the left side of the street. Taxis will only take four passengers. Your driver will expect a minimum 15% tip.

Safety

It's best to abide by a few simple rules of thumb during your visit to New York City. Be careful, don't engage in long conversations with strangers, avoid long, empty city blocks that look dangerous, bypass the subway after dark, and never, ever play hero. It's a good idea to leave valuable jewellery back home or in the hotel safe, use travellers cheques when and where you can, and carry your camera in your handbag. In other words, use your common sense and you'll be fine.

It may happen that a panhandler will approach you, asking for money. It's probably best just to ignore him. If you do opt to give money, drop the change in the cup and move on quickly. (Always keep a few coins handy in your pocket, so you don't have to rummage around in your bag or wallet.)

Don't be afraid of New York: whatever scare stories you may have read, the fact is that the crime rate is the lowest in 30 years, due in large part to former mayor Giuliani's efforts and increased police presence. And keep in mind that some 1.5 million people live, work, play, eat, sleep and raise their children on the island of Manhattan.

Telephones

You will never have a problem finding a coin-operated public telephones. A quarter will get you three minutes locally. Each additional minute requires an extra deposit.

If you're dialling within Manhattan, there's no need to use the area code (212). Just drop the quarter in and dial the 7-digit number. If you're calling Brooklyn, Queens, the Bronx or Staten Island from Manhattan, dial 1, then the area code (718), then the 7-digit number. A recorded voice will tell you how much to deposit (usually 50 cents for the first three minutes). Directory assistance is 411, from whom you can also obtain an address.

For long distance calls in the US outside New York City, dial 1, then the area code, then the 7-digit number. To call the UK from anywhere in the US, dial 011 44, the area code and the local number.

To speak with an international operator, dial 00. To speak to a local operator (if you're having trouble completing a call), dial 0. And always remember, for an emergency just dial 911.

Taxes

There is an 8.5% sales tax on all clothing and food and a 19% tax on hotel rooms.

Time

The 24-hour clock is only used in the US by the military services. Otherwise, the US sticks relentlessly to a.m. and p.m.

New York is on Eastern Standard Time, GMT –5 (with daylight saving time from April to October, GMT – 4).

Tipping

While tipping isn't mandatory, it would be extremely unorthodox to forego it, especially at a restaurant—waiters count on tips to earn a decent wage. The customary tipping rate is 15–20%. An easy way to figure out the proper tip for a meal is to double the tax and, if you're feeling generous, add a dollar or two. Cloakroom attendants will expect $1 per coat, hotel maids $1 a day and porters $2. Room service waiters and taxi drivers should receive 15–20%.

Toilets

Public toilets are something of a rarity in Manhattan. You can find them in Penn Station and Grand Central Station, but they're not always clean, and tend to attract the homeless. Best to use the "restrooms", as the Americans call them, in the lobbies of the larger hotels, big department stores, bookstores or coffeehouses. Restaurants allow only patrons to use their restrooms, but in diners you can gain access to the WC simply by ordering a cup of coffee.

Tourist Information Office

NYC&Co, 810 Seventh Ave at 53rd St. Tel. (212) 484-1222, provides extensive information on guided tours, restaurants, museums, sightseeing, shopping, children's activities and transportation. You can stop by the Bureau for a Visitor's Packet.

Before your trip, it's worth exploring the web site at: http://www.nycvisit.com for up-to-date information on sights and entertainment.

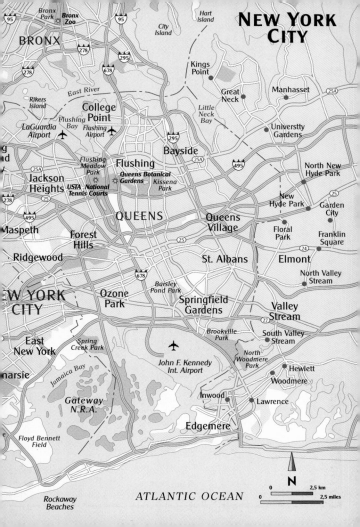

GREENWICH VILLAGE

East 14th Street
East 13th Street
East 12th Street
East 11th Street

St. Marks-In-The-Bowery

Third Avenue

East 10th Street
East 9th Street

Stuyvesant St

East 8th Street
East 7th Street
East 6th Street
East 5th Street
East 4th Street
East 3rd Street
East 2nd Street
East 1st Street
East Houston Street

Second Avenue

Grace Church

Bowery
Broadway

Astor Pl.

Cooper Square

Lafayette St.

EAST VILLAGE

Bowery

Elizabeth St.
Mott St.
Mulberry St.
Lafayette St.
Crosby St.

First Presbyterian Church

Church of the Ascension

East 10th Street
East 9th Street

West 11th Street
West 10th Street
West 9th Street

East 8th Street

Fifth Avenue

Washington Mews

University Pl.

Washington Square North

Waverly Place

Washington Pl.

Broadway

Great Jones St.
Bond Street
Bleecker St.

Kenmare

MacDougal Alley

Washington Square Park

East 8th Street

East 4th Street

New York University

Washington Square Village

University Plaza

Mercer St.

Guggenheim SoHo

Wooster St.

West 8th Street

Washington Square Arch

Washington Square South

Student Center

Loeb

Bobst Library

La Guardia Pl.

Bleecker St.

West Houston Street

SoHo

Broadway

Patchin Pl.

Village Square

Avenue of the Americas

Waverly Place

Washington Place

West

Judson Memorial Church

Thompson St.

Sullivan St.

MacDougal St.

WEST VILLAGE

Sheridan Square

Seventh Ave.

Grove St.

Christopher Street

West 10th Street

Perry Street

Charles Street

Sixth Avenue

Bedford Street

Commerce St.

Barrow St.

Morton Street

Bleecker Street

Father Demo Square

Carmine St.

Downing St.

Seventh Avenue

Leroy St.

Hudson Street

James J. Walker Park

Clarkson St.

Houston Street

King St.

Charlton Street

Vandam Street

Spring St.

Ave. of the Americas

Father Fagan Park

SOHO

Varick Street

Greenwich Street

Holland

N

Abyssinian Baptist Church 45
Alice Austen House and Garden 49
American Ballet Theatre 61
American Craft Museum 33–34
American Museum of Natural History 43
Antiques 36
Bars 62–63
Battery Park 17
Bergdorf Goodman 32
Bloomingdales 32
Bronx 46
Bronx Zoo 46
Brooklyn 47–48
Brooklyn Botanic Garden 48
Brooklyn Bridge 17
Brooklyn Museum of Art 48
Bryant Park 30
Carl Schurtz Park 38
Carnegie Hall 61
Castle Clinton 18
Cathedral of St John the Divine 43–44
Central Park 35
Chelsea 26
Children's Museum of the Arts 21–22
Chinatown 20
Christie's New York 32
Chrysler Building 28

Church of the Ascension 24
Church of the Transfiguration 21
City Hall 14
City Tours 19
Cloisters 45
Contemporary music 63–64
Cooper-Hewitt Museum 40
Danceland 65
Duane Park 22
East Village 25
El Museo del Barrio 41
Ellis Island Immigration Museum 18
Empire State Building 27
F.A.O. Schwarz 32
Federal Hall National Memorial 16
First Shearith Israel Graveyard 20
Flatiron Building 26
Flea markets 36
Fraunces Tavern Museum 15
Frick Collection 37
George Washington Bridge 45
Grace Church 25
Grand Central Terminal 28–30
Greenwich Village 23–24
Ground Zero 15

Guggenheim Museum 39
- SoHo 23
Harlem 44
Henri Bendell 32
Historic Richmond Town 49
International Center of Photography 40
International Wildlife Conservation Park 46
Intrepid Sea-Air-Space Museum 30–31
Jacques Marchais Museum of Tibetan Art 49
Jazz and blues clubs 64–65
Jefferson Market Library 24
Jewish Museum 40
Knoedler & Co 37
Lincoln Center 42
Little Italy 21
Macy's 32
Madison Square Garden 27
Mary Boone 33
Merchant's House Museum 25–26
Metropolitan Museum of Art 38–39
Metropolitan Opera House 61
Morningside Heights 43

Museum of Modern
   Art 34
– of Radio
   and Television 33
– of the Chinese
   Americans 20
– of the City of New
   York 41
National Lighthouse
   Museum 49
National Museum of
   the American
   Indian 18
New York Botanical
   Gardens 46
New York City
   Ballet 62
– Fire Museum 23
– Library 20
– Opera 62
New York
   Philharmonic 62
– Police
   Headquarters 21
– Stock Exchange 16
Old St Patrick's
   Cathedral 21
PaceWildenstein
   MacGill 34
Prospect Park 48
Queens 46–47
Queensboro Bridge
   36
Radio City Music
   Hall 32
Riverside Park 43
Rockefeller Center
   31
Saks Fifth Ave 32

Shopping 32
SoHo 23
Sotheby's 37
South Street Seaport
   Museum 16–17
St Mark's Church in
   the Bowery 26
St Patrick's Cathedral
   32–33
Staten Island 49
Statue of Liberty 19
Studio Museum in
   Harlem 44-45
Tiffany 32
Times Square 31
Tompkins Square 25
TriBeCa 22
Trinity Church 15–16
Trump Tower 34
Union Square
   Greenmarket 26
United Nations 27–28
Upper East Side
   35–36
Upper West Side 41
Verrazano-Narrows
   Bridge 49
Vietnam Veterans
   Memorial 17
Wall Street 14–15
Washington Market
   Park 23
Washington Square
   24–25
Whitney Museum of
   American Art 37–38
Wildlife Center 48
Woolworth Building
   14

GENERAL EDITOR
Barbara Ender-Jones
RESEARCH
Dorsey Smith
Diana Niles King
LAYOUT
Alain Piccard
PHOTO CREDITS
Mediacom S. A.: front cover;
Christine Osborne Pictures,
inside front cover,
pp. 8–9, 42;
Hémisphères/Rieger,
pp. 1, 10, 22, 29, 39, 47, 60;
Hémisphères/Giraudou, p. 5;
Jean Mohr, p. 2;
Neil Setchfield, p. 53
MAPS
Elsner & Schichor;
Subway Map,
© MTA Metropolitan
Transportation Authority

Copyright © 2002, 1998
by JPM Publications S.A.
12, avenue William-Fraisse,
1006 Lausanne, Switzerland
information@jpmguides.com
http://www.jpmguides.com/

Printed in Switzerland
Weber/Bienne (CTP) — 02/07/01